Questions and *Answers* About Your Journey to God

Fr. Benedict J. Groeschel, C.F.R.

Questions and *Answers* About Your Journey to God

Our Sunday Visitor Publishing Division
Our Sunday Visitor, Inc.
Huntington, Indiana 46750

CONTENTS

FOREWORD

More than twenty years ago, I attended a retreat given by Fr. Benedict Groeschel. It was based on a book that he had recently published with Crossroad Publishing entitled *Spiritual Passages*. The retreat was absolutely, without reservation, the best retreat I had ever attended. Father Benedict opened up a treasure house of Catholic spirituality to my fellow retreatants and me.

Ever since I became an acquisitions editor for Our Sunday Visitor in the late 1990s, it has been a personal dream of mine for Father Benedict to write a book for us that will provide simple answers to the questions that people, like me, are often confronted with as we make our way along our pilgrimage toward God. Thankfully, Father has agreed to take me up on this offer.

Father Benedict says in one of the answers in this book: "I decided decades ago that my speaking and preaching would largely be an attempt at spiritual direction given to groups." In this book, Father accomplishes this in a very direct way, by answering questions. Many of the questions were derived from a large group of people who were asked to submit questions that they would like Father Benedict to answer about the spiritual life. These people were responding to a query posted on my online blog, Annunciations. Other questions were my own, and still others were added by Father Benedict to reflect what people have asked him over his many years of giving spiritual direction.

As this book was being completed, I visited Father Benedict at Trinity Retreat House in New York. He was in the midst of giving a retreat to priests and graciously allowed me to sit in on one of the conferences. It was an uplifting talk on the virtue of hope.

There was one line that struck me in Father's talk, a line he repeated several times: "Hope is ultimately an expectation for eternal life."

The spiritual life is hope-filled because we, unlike those without faith, expect to live forever. Archbishop Bruno Forte has said it well: "Life is either a pilgrimage or a foretaste of death." Thanks be to God for giving us the faith so that our life is a journey toward Him!

May the answers Father Benedict provides in this book give you great hope and help you navigate your way toward the Lord every day of your life — and, ultimately, for all eternity.

Michael Dubruiel
Feast of the Visitation of Mary
May 31, 2007

Part One

THE SPIRITUAL LIFE

I.

THE LIFE OF THE SPIRIT

✦ **What do we mean by the term the "spiritual life"?**

This expression is widely used to describe that aspect of someone's life which is pointed toward realities that are intangible — things that cannot be seen or touched — and it is used by those of different religions and points of view.

Christians use the term to mean that aspect of our life that seeks God and tries to come to greater knowledge or possession of Him. Christians do this by following Christ's example. Because Christ is God and a Person of the Holy Trinity, we want to come closer to Him and know Him better. In a sense we try to establish an intimate relationship with Him, which is possible only through grace, the gift of His love. Therefore, the Christian spiritual life is the life of grace: "[A]part from me you can do nothing" (John 15:5).

✦ **How is it possible to have an intimate relationship with Christ?**

It seems clear that Our Lord invites us to such a relationship: "If a man loves me, he will keep my word, and my Father will love him, and we will come to him and make our home with him" (John 14:23). "Behold, I stand at the door and knock; if any one hears my voice and opens the door, I will come in to him and eat with him, and he with me" (Revelation 3:20); He also says, "Come to me, all who labor and are heavy laden, and I will give you rest. Take my yoke upon you, and learn from me; for I am gentle and lowly in heart, and you will find rest for your souls. For my yoke is easy, and my burden is light" (Matthew 11:28–30). Finally He says, "I am with you always, to the close of the age" (Matthew 28:20). All of this invites us to a personal spiritual life, one that relates intimately with God through His Son.

✦ **Does the spiritual life differ from the rest of a person's life, or is there only one life, of which the spiritual is very much a part?**

Each of us is only one person. A human being is a union of body and soul, of matter and spirit. We act on many different levels. Each level can be called a life of its own. We have a physical life of the body. Many people have a married life, a single life. We can speak of the intellectual life. When we speak of a person's attention and behavior that pertain to the following of Christ and the possession of God, we call it the spiritual life.

✦ **Is there a spiritual life that is common to all men and women regardless of their beliefs?**

It has traditionally been Church teaching that there is a universal call to holiness, or to the deep possession of God through the mind and soul. Consequently, we can say that in one way there is a common spiritual life. However, because of different religious and spiritual beliefs, people live out that reality differently. A devout Buddhist, for example, seeking to come closer to God will lead a certain kind of spiritual life, and the same would be true of followers of other religions. However, my own personal experience suggests that all who have made genuine progress on the journey to God and whose spiritual life deeply affects their daily existence have something in common. They usually know a peacefulness because their life is centered on one reality. They have a sense of quiet in prayer or contemplation because the reality they consider most important is not of the changing physical world. Generally speaking, I have also found that those who struggle with spiritual growth in different religions and cultures are kindly people who show deference and respect for others, even those with whom they disagree. I have often travelled in the Far East and visited shrines and monasteries of other religions. I have always been courteously received at such places and have noticed that in one way or another we are all walking on parallel paths toward God.

✦ **How is the spiritual life of a Christian different from that of those who do not follow Christianity?**

The most important difference between Christianity and other world religions — even Judaism, from which our religion grows — is that we follow God as He suffered. We are the religion of the suffering God. In our churches there should be a crucifix. The sign of Christ is the Cross, a sign of terrible punishment and dereliction that has been transformed into a sign of hope.

For this reason a Christian is willing to suffer and endure things in order to grow closer to God in the spiritual life. People of other religions also suffer, but they do not have the incredible example of a suffering God. They may have the idea of enduring difficulties and sufferings as a form of worship and dedication and acceptance of the divine will. Obviously, they would do painful things like fasting in order to accomplish God's will and, I assume, offer that as a prayer. There is no way for them, however, to identify with the sufferings of God. Christianity is the religion of the God who weeps, who struggles, who falls on the pavement, who cries out in agony, and who dies offering Himself to the heavenly Father. That is what makes Christianity so obviously different. Added to that immediately is the glorious triumph of Jesus Christ in His Resurrection. The belief in the Incarnation, the passion, and the Resurrection, therefore, is what makes the Christian spiritual life different.

✦ **Is there such a thing as "one-size-fits-all" spirituality?**

When we get down to brass tacks, each person obviously leads a very personal spiritual life, walking on a personal spiritual path. Many others may be walking along with us, but each one, being unique, has his or her own path to walk. In a monastery, even in my own community of friars and sisters, all the members have the same goals, ideals, models, and purposes. Each one, however, is on a slightly different path and definitely in a different place. It is perhaps best to think of the spiritual journey as a series of parallel paths leading to God, with each person in his or her own place on that path.

✦ **Is psychology (which means the "study of the spirit") a scientific effort to explore the spiritual life? How has it influenced the modern view of the spiritual life?**

In modern times, especially in the twentieth century, there has been an effort to apply psychology to the spiritual life. This was understandable, since psychology and psychotherapy were important in the lives of people in Western civilization. Much of the rest of the world, except the Japanese, remained largely untouched by the speculations of the great twentieth-century psychologists. Some of the first modern psychologists, like Freud, were atheists with no interest in the spiritual life. Some were eclectic students of religion and spirituality, like Carl Gustav Jung, and at times they studied the spiritual life directly, often without any effort to embrace it themselves. Those who most seriously attempted to look at the psychology of the spiritual life were spiritual writers who had some knowledge or training in psychology. My book *Spiritual Passages* was an attempt to relate psychological theories of human development to the descriptions of the spiritual journey given by the classic authors of the spiritual life.

✦ What is meant by the "Ways" in the spiritual life?

Early in Christian history people used the idea of a journey, with stages along the way, to illustrate what happens in the spiritual life. After all, Christ said, "Follow me." Two of them were contemporaries, but they never read each other's books, because one wrote in Greek and the other in Latin. They were Saint Gregory of Nyssa, a Greek bishop, and Saint Augustine, a bishop in North Africa and one of the greatest minds of Western civilization. Saint Augustine's *Confessions*, in particular, is an attempt to apply an understanding of human life to the life of the spirit. Questions he raises in his books and answers he gives are still posed in books in modern times. He is referred to in the history of psychology as the "holy psychologist."

Later on in the Church, remarkable people like Saints Bonaventure, Teresa of Avila, and John of the Cross also studied the life of the spirit from what we would call a psychological point of view. They were brilliant psychologists who observed, compared, described, accepted or rejected various psychological experiences of God and of the Christian life. Writers in the Muslim and Jewish world did the same thing.

In our time this kind of effort has often been much affected by the psychology that was popular at the moment because it was of interest to people. As one of those who tried to make a synthesis of spiritual doctrine and contemporary psychological theory, it seems to me that this process is like building a wall of mortar and granite blocks. The granite blocks were the truths in the Gospel, Scriptures, Church tradition, experience of the saints; the mortar was contemporary psychological theory. Anyone who has maintained a stone wall knows that sooner or later that mortar grows old and wears away, and the stone has to be pointed, or perhaps rebuilt.

✦ **Has psychology been a good influence in the spiritual life?**

Sometimes yes, and sometimes no. Unfortunately, in the 1970s and 1980s various theories in psychology that were fundamentally wrong philosophically and theologically gave rise to very popular ideas in Christianity and in the life of the clergy. The teaching of Carl Rogers that you would be healthy if you just expressed all your inner feelings and conflicts and got what you wanted, and became your total self, was quite contrary to Christian teaching. It revived an error going back to Pelagius, a fifth-century monk, who taught that there was no original sin and that we have within ourselves the necessary ingredients for our salvation. Pelagius maintained that Christ showed us the right road to salvation, and we proceed with our own energy. This thinking, which was particularly identified with nondirective therapy, did great harm, in my opinion, to the spiritual lives of many. Nevertheless, a number of fine dedicated Catholic writers and teachers, like Charles A. Curran, George Hagmeier, and my esteemed teacher Brother John Egan, C.F.C., attempted to baptize Rogers' theory and were able to help many people more with psychological rather than with spiritual problems.

Ideas related to governing one's thoughts in a healthy way or cognitive theory have recently taken over much of clinical psychology and psychotherapy. Leaders in the field of psychotherapy, and particularly some officers of the American Psychological Association, have now identified mental health with the development of virtue and character strengths. This is an astonishing development; unfortunately, it has yet to have much impact in the Christian world. It is interesting to note that when leaders in this field, led by Dr. Martin Seligman, tried to find a definition of virtue — something that psychology cannot provide — they turned to the Scriptures, to philosophers like Plato and Aristotle, and to Saints Augustine and Thomas Aquinas.[1]

As a result of the new emphasis on virtue, a number of popular theories ought to be redone in contemporary writing on psychology and spirituality. Christians, Catholics included, are, quite frankly, a bit behind the times.

✦ Is there a difference between New Age spiritualities and Christian spirituality?

To put it bluntly, it is like the difference between hell and heaven, or at least between purgatory and heaven. "New Age–type spiritualities" is a very vague term. Anyone can identify with the New Age. It generally becomes a collection of untried theories, shaky ideas, and the glitter of the passing moment. Christian spirituality has a tradition of two thousand years, while Jewish and Buddhist spirituality is three thousand years old. To think that one can float on top of the water without any real relationship to the past is what I would think deserves to be called foolishness. Some people in the New Age, however, do look back selectively to the traditions of the past, although on a smorgasbord basis. They pick out what they like. Many things in the classic writers on the spiritual life, whether Christian or not, present people with challenges. It is not all happy news. Those who do not want to face unpleasant things about themselves with a view toward improving them should not get involved with the spiritual life.

New Age spirituality does appeal to a certain real element of the human personality that looks for the transcendent or at least for what is not diminished by time. Most human needs and experiences will find an echo in the spiritual writings of world religions. The trouble is that New Agers do not follow any basic theology or organized system of thought. Devotees of the New Age will pick out what appeals to them. It is an almost infallible way of following a path of spiritual detours.

The New Age, however, can lead at times to another, more authentic approach to God. I have met a number of people who, starting with little or no Christian faith, became involved with the New Age, found it unconvincing, and moved on to orthodox

Christian teaching and Catholic spiritual life. That is not so unusual, and it is a pleasure to see. On the other hand, Catholics and other Christians who are lukewarm or whose faith is crumbling away may find some solace and self-importance in New Age spirituality. Sad examples of this abound. Their situation becomes a spiritual disaster, as they reject the teachings of the Gospel of the Son of God for highly subjective selections from the spiritual experiences of many cultures and traditions. They deny, implicitly or explicitly, that Christ is the Son of God and Savior of the world. Perhaps they never really believed it but were sociologically involved in a Christian culture without any real faith.

✦ **Can we learn anything from non-Christian spiritual writings?**

I have often enjoyed and learned things from other spiritualities, but always from the viewpoint of the Gospel. Jesus says: "And I have other sheep, that are not of this fold; I must bring them also, and they will heed my voice" (John 10:16). Saint Paul, speaking to the Athenians, cites other spiritualities when he says: "'In him we live and move and have our being'" (Acts 17:28). This means that someone who is solidly and personally dedicated to the Christian faith is able to recognize how God and His grace calls those who have not had the blessing of Christian Baptism and faith. However, to reject the uniqueness of the Gospel and belief in Christ for a fruit salad of different observations on the spiritual life — some of them valuable, others questionable or just silly, many others just self-indulgent of human passions — is a road to disaster. Jesus, the Good Shepherd, tells us not to listen to the deceiver who will lead us astray, but to listen to His voice, the voice of truth, as sheep listen to the shepherd's voice. The shepherd:

> "... goes before them, and the sheep follow him, for
> they know his voice. A stranger they will not follow, but

they will flee from him, for they do not know the voice of strangers" (John 10:4–5).

He warns us against those who would come and scatter the flock of God.

"He who is a hireling and not a shepherd, whose own the sheep are not, sees the wolf coming and leaves the sheep and flees; and the wolf snatches them and scatters them. He flees because he is a hireling and cares nothing for the sheep" (John 10:12–13).

✦ Isn't the spiritual life just for priests and nuns?

By no means. In fact, almost quite the contrary. The spiritual life is for every soul created by God. Clergy and religious form a group within the universal population who are called to take the spiritual life very seriously. However, some of the great spiritual people of all religions were laypeople, or at least started out as laypeople. Obviously they reached a degree of real spiritual development before they became clergy or religious. Examples of great lay spiritual giants include Catherine of Siena, the mystic who died at the age of thirty-three after having persuaded the Pope to return to Rome from Avignon; and Catherine of Genoa, who began the whole process of the Catholic Reformation at the end of the fifteenth century; and the devout Protestant layman Dag Hammarskjöld, Secretary-General of the United Nations, who wrote a profound spiritual diary. Examples of those who were advanced on the spiritual way before they became priests or religious include Saints Francis of Assisi, Ignatius of Loyola, and Elizabeth Seton. No one is exempt from the call of God. The lives of priests and religious, however, will usually be arranged to accommodate more easily the pursuit of spiritual things. At least that is how it is supposed to be.

✦ **How would you characterize some of the schools of Catholic spirituality (i.e., Benedictine, Dominican, and Franciscan)? How do I know which is for me?**

In the course of the centuries certain great spiritual leaders who began religious orders fostered spiritual programs that were distinctive to themselves. This was usually shown by the kind of religious community they established or led. In the fifth century, for example, a Roman gentleman stepped out of the declining society and founded an order of monks. There were already monks in the Church, but he began a distinctive type of monastic tradition — simple, liturgical, fraternal and communal, and open to many kinds of work that did not disturb the monk's inner life. This was Saint Benedict of Nursia. The influence of his monks down the ages has been incalculable. It can be said that Saint Benedict's monks saved civilization in Western Europe. Today he is the patron saint of Europe and, for that reason, the chosen patron of Pope Benedict XVI.

Saint Dominic belonged to a group of canons regular, but he chose to adopt a more humble and apostolic life dedicated especially to preaching. The large number of Dominican communities — friars, sisters, and lay tertiaries — have their own spiritual outlook, often deeply influenced by Saint Thomas Aquinas, who is their most eminent theologian and writer on the spiritual life.

Saint Francis, on the other hand, was not a priest or religious, but a layman whose incredible spiritual experiences led him to try to follow Christ as literally as possible. He brought to the task his unique personality, captivated by goodness and beauty. A group of disciples quickly gathered round him, and that was the beginning of the Franciscan order, with its many saints, branches, and twigs. The Franciscans of the Renewal, to which I belong, are one of those twigs.

Each of these groups has a unique flavor, as do many other schools of spirituality. However, all follow the basic outline of the spiritual life known as the three ways, which we will examine. Most laypeople will not be attracted to any one of the schools we have mentioned, but will simply have their own direct following of the Gospel. The schools are meant only as a help or guide. Fundamentally there is only one spiritual way: to follow Jesus and respond to His call, "Follow me."

✦ **How does the spiritual life involve both interior dispositions and exterior actions?**

Since human beings are a union, rather than a combination, of body and spirit, they must act in an integrated way. World religions, especially the Scriptures of Judaism and Christianity, as well as the life of Christ, make clear that our external actions must be in accord with inner beliefs. This is obvious in the Sermon on the Mount and the parables, which are the collection of moral teachings of Our Lord. In fact, He was critical of those who did not translate their beliefs into behavior with personal dedication and sacrifice. At times people appear to be attracted to Oriental spirituality, which is presented in such a way that it does not affect external behavior except for a withdrawal into silence. This is quite unfair to Oriental spirituality and, at best, a misunderstanding of it. I have met people of different non-Christian spiritualities. I cannot say that I ever met one who thought their external behavior should not be determined by inner belief. This would be hypocrisy.

✦ **Can we be spiritual without being religious, without going to church?**

Spirituality is a relationship with God. Of its essence it must be individual, personal, and interior. Jesus said, "If a man loves me, he will keep my word, and my Father will love him, and we will come to him and make our home with him" (John 14:23).

On the other hand, religion is an external, social phenomenon with profound roots in the human personality, which means that it is an anthropological reality. No matter where we go in the world, we will always find religion. In modern times people have attempted to stamp out religion, but they have been noticeably unsuccessful. For this reason religion is a moral virtue, which is generally recognized by all unprejudiced human beings. Even in anti-religious times — for instance, under Communism and Nazism — we find profoundly spiritual and religious people operating quietly underground.

Religion and spirituality come together in Christianity. Christ was not only the spiritual light of the human race; He is also the founder of His own Church. He speaks of His Church, saying: "[O]n this rock I will build my church" (Matthew 16:18). He also tells the apostles, whom He appointed as leaders of His Church, that those who listen to them listen to Him (see Luke 10:16). He says in St. John's Gospel that the Holy Spirit will lead them to all truth (see John 16:13). Since the early days of Christianity, beginning with Saint Paul, profound spirituality has accompanied zeal and fervor for the Church. One has only to read Saint Paul, who had not actually known or seen Our Lord during His earthly life, to realize that religion, spirituality, and Christianity are inseparable.

✦ **Does a truly spiritual person need external religion?**

In the Church's history and tradition it is demonstrable that none of its great spiritual figures down the ages have dispensed themselves from the responsibility of the external practice of their faith. This is true even of people like Joan of Arc, who was persecuted by Church authorities and is nonetheless a canonized saint.

Unfortunately, not all Church leaders or clergy are as spiritual as the laypeople who look to them for spiritual guidance. That was a problem in the Old Testament and has continued to be one in Christian history. In the light of all that, a spiritual person must ultimately come to decision: Do I accept the means of worship and salvation, especially the sacraments, which Christ has established? If not, we are on our own, which is a very dangerous and chilly place to be. Although we may be interested in the spiritual life, we may not be particularly inclined to external religious practices. But where would spirituality be without external religion to support it? There is the inescapable fact that Christ Himself established these external signs as sacraments, especially Baptism and the Holy Eucharist.

✦ How does a spiritual person gain from being a Catholic?

The Catholic Church has the world's greatest library of spiritual literature, as well as the greatest identifiable collection of splendid spiritual teachers and canonized saints. In our age, as in every other, it has presented magnificent spiritual models to the human race. In the twentieth century alone we have seen Mother Teresa and Pope John Paul II, along with many others. In New York City alone, there are at least seven people proposed for beatification.

Along with getting many blessings from the Church, beginning with Christ's sacraments, which of themselves cause grace, we also receive the opportunity to serve others in the Church. It is the entrée to all kinds of works of charity. In the fifth century a number of people withdrew into solitude and eremitical life as the Roman civilization was coming apart. Violence and scandal were everywhere. They were called anchorites. The Church Fathers, who led the Church at the time and were great theologians and spiritual writers, did not like or trust the anchorites. One of the best known of the Fathers and a sacramental theologian, Saint Ambrose, archbishop of Milan, wrote to the anchorites, asking them that if they lived alone, whose burdens would they carry, and in relation to whom would they take the lowest place.

Some people in our society pretend to be spiritual without belonging to a Christian community. Chances are good that they will learn the hard way. They will become either discouraged or eccentric. While it can be a burden or a distraction to belong to the external body of the Church, it is a fulfillment of the natural law of religion and the divine law of faith. Spirituality, according to Christ, should not be attempted alone. The danger is that we may end up worshipping an image of ourselves rather than the living God.

✦ **Are there any methods or efforts from Protestant or Eastern Orthodox Christianity that are useful for Catholics in the spiritual life?**

Of course there are. They can be discovered by reading some important and helpful books written by Orthodox and Protestant Christians. Within the next year I hope to publish a book on the history of devotion to Our Lord Jesus Christ in all three branches of Christianity.

Since Eastern Orthodox Christians share with Catholics almost all the truths of faith, their writings are particularly helpful to us. Pope John Paul II referred to the branches, East and West, as the two lungs of the Church. Many Catholics have found the writings of eastern mystics helpful in the spiritual life. In the Orthodox writings we find a great sense of the meaning of the Church and of sanctifying grace, of the significance of the liturgy in the spiritual life, and of devotion to the Blessed Virgin.

Protestant spiritual writers are slightly more difficult for Catholics. Certain key elements of Catholic spirituality related to the sacraments, especially the Eucharist, and the saints are missing, as well as some other things. However, this is not the case with certain Anglican writers, like Evelyn Underhill. Among Protestant writers, many give great testimony to devotion to Christ and the importance of being His disciple. We all experience the tragedies of life together, and we all read the same Bible and go to the same Lord in prayer. I have found much wisdom in certain Protestant spiritual writers, especially modern writers like Dietrich Bonhoeffer, Dag Hammarskjöld, and Elisabeth Elliot, to name only a few.

✦ **Is there such a thing as a goal in the spiritual life?**

Yes, but I hesitate to use that word, which has become part of various human enterprises and struggles, for example, financial and other material goals. The spiritual life is ultimately God working within us. If we think of it as a goal of our own work, we move toward the heresy of Pelagianism. Pelagius was a fifth-century Irish monk who denied original sin and who taught that Jesus saves us only by His teaching and by leading us on the way to God. Ultimately, he denied the necessity of grace. His teaching was first condemned at the Council of Ephesus (431). His great critic was Saint Augustine.

Unfortunately, a watered-down version of Pelagianism is still with us. It is properly called semi-Pelagianism, and it is seen in all attempts to minimize the necessity of God's grace either explicitly or implicitly.

II.

AIDS TO LIVING A SPIRITUAL LIFE

✦ **Is there only one way of living the spiritual life?**

People who seriously attempt to live a spiritual life sometimes come to the conclusion that their way is the best or only way. It may be the best for them. There are general norms for the spiritual life that all Christians try to follow, like the Sermon on the Mount and the parables. If we try with trust and faith to follow Christ as He speaks in the Gospel, we will lead a truly Christian life no matter what school of the spiritual life we are drawn to.

✦ **Are there methods of prayer everyone should practice?**

The term "methods of prayer" is used in many ways, usually to describe different approaches to meditation. Everyone is called to certain tasks of prayer, which include praying at the liturgy with faith, reverence, and awe, and a prayerful reading of Sacred Scripture and other spiritual books, like lives of the saints. We are also called to private and personal prayer, and to devotional prayer like the Rosary and the Stations of the Cross. Spiritual fulfillment may vary at times, including different types of prayer. It is helpful to keep in mind the advice of an English monk, Dom John Chapman: "Pray as you can; don't pray as you can't."

✦ **Some people find it difficult to pray the Rosary or similar devotions? What should we do if we find certain spiritual practices, prayers, or devotions not to our liking?**

The saints tell us that feelings should count for little or nothing in the spiritual life. We should never abandon devotional prayers completely; instead, we should struggle, if we have to, to say them well — for example, the Rosary. We should also study how to pray the Rosary well; it is not obvious. There are books on how to pray the Rosary well. The same is true of the Stations of the Cross. Devotions that are not a standard part of Catholic piety can be chosen as our need or inclination suggests. Certain enthusiasts for a particular devotion frequently decide that the rest of the world must follow their lead. This is a bit silly. The very reason for private devotion is to allow people to choose the ones most meaningful to them. Some devotions, like those to the Sacred Heart of Jesus, the Divine Mercy, or the Blessed Virgin Mary, have universal approval. Other devotions may depend on individual needs.

✦ What role do the Mass and sacraments play in spiritual growth?

For Catholics and Orthodox Christians sacramental prayer is of the greatest importance because Christ speaks to us and prays with us in the Church's liturgy and sacramental life. In recent times some Catholics have come to think of the Mass as a group activity, something that must be found engaging. This has led to what Pope Benedict XVI has called the "collapse of the liturgy," which has occurred because liturgical changes were sometimes made based on what was thought to be engaging or even entertaining. Liturgical prayer should always be done with awe and reverence and the knowledge that Christ is praying with us.[2]

✦ What role do Our Lady and the saints play in the spiritual life?

Our Lady is a model of prayer for us, particularly her New Testament prayer, the *Magnificat*. Her whole life, in fact, must be seen as a prayer of obedience and trust in God, especially her accompanying Christ to His crucifixion and death. The saints show us how to persevere amid intense trials and disappointments. We sometimes think that the saints' prayers must have been works of great beauty, like symphonies, but often they reveal much struggle, suffering, and trust. The prayerful poems of Saint Thérèse of Lisieux provide us with an excellent example, but they should be read along with her autobiography,[3] which reveals great trials and suffering.

✦ Should we have an established routine of daily prayer?

Routine in life is a protection against confusion and idleness. It makes for a productive life, and prayer should take its place among a regular schedule of eating, sleeping, and work. I have learned in a busy urban life that the best prayer time is either early morning or late evening. It is good to fix that and get some prayer time in the middle of the day. Praying early is particularly helpful. I read once that in New York the best revenge is getting up early. Pausing to pray at specific times during the day helps to keep our minds and hearts fixed on God. The ancient custom of the Angelus, the prayer of the Incarnation, is a good practice to cultivate, as are visits to a church or chapel to adore Christ present in the Holy Eucharist, or simply to pray if the Eucharist is not present.

✦ What is the daily examen? Is it a necessary part of spiritual growth?

The examen refers to an examination of conscience, in which we take a moral inventory of our lives and actions each day and arrive at an honest appraisal of how we are doing.

Without being scrupulous, we should look at our most obvious failures and also try to see things we may have overlooked as obligations, for example, the care of the poor. At the end of each examen we should always resolve to do better and ask for God's mercy and forgiveness.

✦ **Is the spiritual life something suited more to the introvert than to the extrovert?**

The terms "introvert" and "extrovert" indicate psychological categories that are not especially accurate descriptions of most people. In general terms it can be said that either tendency can be helpful in the spiritual life. Those who tend to be introverted, or quiet, will find certain forms of prayers helpful, whereas the more extroverted will find works of charity and kindness easier to perform. We have interesting examples of the two differing types in recent history: Mother Teresa, a somewhat introverted, or interior, person, and Padre Pio, who by all accounts was a moderate extrovert. God takes us and uses us where we are.

✦ **How can we judge whether we are growing in the spiritual life? Are there danger signs to indicate we are moving in the wrong direction?**

This is a difficult question because as we make progress in the spiritual life, it will seem to us that we are going backwards. We should be wary rather of those who think they are making progress. Many saints have said that as we grow in the spiritual life, we learn increasingly how far we are from God, although in fact we are growing closer to Him. Our Lord tells us that in order to enter the kingdom of heaven, we must become like little children (see Matthew 18:3). All serious discussion of spiritual progress must include the idea of spiritual childhood. Without this recognition the big danger becomes pride and self-reliance.

✦ **Is it necessary to have a spiritual director?**[4]

It is helpful for those who take the spiritual life seriously, especially in the early stages, to have a spiritual director. It may be necessary to get a good confessor who can be relied on. A director should be chosen very carefully. Currently a great deal of spiritual direction must be done in groups or with books or tapes due to the dearth of adequate spiritual directors. Because of the large number of people seeking spiritual direction, I decided decades ago that my speaking and preaching would largely be an attempt at spiritual direction given to groups. In that way people could discover what they thought they needed and work on that. Spiritual reading also provides the same guidance.

✦ **Does the frequent reception of the sacrament of Reconciliation and the Holy Eucharist play a role in the spiritual life?**

The saints and others who have made progress in the spiritual life will answer with a resounding yes. The daily, or frequent, prayerful reception of the Holy Eucharist is most important. But the manner in which the Eucharist is received is extraordinarily important because we can go to Communion in an almost perfunctory or mechanical way. Those Christians who do not have the Holy Eucharist as part of their lives should be careful to pause and acknowledge Christ's presence in their lives and hearts by His grace. We all need to see that He and the Father dwell within us by the power of the Holy Spirit. This realization is extremely important in the spiritual life.

The sacrament of Reconciliation is a wonderful way to check oneself and also to receive the sacramental grace of the Lord's forgiveness. Confession makes our estimation of our own sins very real and personal.

✦ **Is there a recognized path of development in the spiritual life?**

Yes, and it is called the road (or doctrine) of the three ways. It is first spoken of by Saint Augustine in the fifth century, as well as by his near contemporary, Saint Gregory of Nyssa. The doctrine was expanded considerably by Saint Bonaventure (1221–1274), and new insights were given in the sixteenth century by Saint Teresa of Avila and Saint John of the Cross. In the course of history many classic spiritual writers contributed to the understanding of the three ways, which are: 1) the Purgative, or purification; 2) the Illuminative, or growth in the knowledge and love of God; and 3) the Unitive, or transformation by God and His grace. In modern times, the doctrine has been elaborated especially by Père Garrigou-Lagrange's book *The Three Ways of the Interior Life*. I wrote extensively about the psychology of this road in my book *Spiritual Passages*.[5]

Part Two

THE JOURNEY TO GOD

THE THREE WAYS OF THE SPIRITUAL LIFE

Awakening	Purgative			Illuminative			Unitive			
	Moral Con-version	Mature Faith	Trust in God	First Darkness	Charity to Neighbor	Love of God	Dark Night of the Senses	Simple Union with God	Second Dark Night of the Soul	Trans-forming Union with God
FIRST CONVERSION										
GROWTH IN VIRTUE	Moral Virtues	Faith	Hope	Strengthening of Virtue	Zeal, Kindness, Generosity, Forgiveness	Dedication, Sacrifice, Contemplative Meditation		Gifts of Holy Spirit/ Beginning of Con-templa-tion		Contem-plation/ Simplicity of Prayer

III.

CONVERSION — THE AWAKENING

✦ **What is the place of conversion in the spiritual life?**

It must first be admitted that we never complete our conversion. The whole Christian spiritual life is an act of constant conversion. For that reason the first public words of Jesus are: "The time is fulfilled, and the kingdom of God is at hand; repent, and believe in the gospel" (Mark 1:15). However, there is a time, or even a moment, of intense conversion. This comes when someone has been leading a thoughtless or sinful life without paying attention to God and is unaware of any moral shortcomings. Apparently, out of the blue God will call them to a serious conversion. While some people who have always led a devout life may be less aware of a particular moment of conversion, they will nevertheless recall times when they took a leap in the right direction, when they moved from childish to mature faith, from mediocrity to a serious commitment to pleasing God.

✦ **Some of those who have had experiences in cults or in modern retreat programs have at times been manipulated into an experience of conversion that is purely psychological and quickly fades. How can we distinguish between a true experience of conversion from the Holy Spirit and one that is merely psychological?**

It is possible for people who come under influences that are not specifically Christian to undergo an experience of enlightenment, or sharpening of their awareness of the spiritual. At best, it may be simply an experience of natural religion, of which we spoke earlier. It quickly fades and does not lead to any commitment to the Gospel. Others may have a genuine Christian conversion occasioned by a powerful experience that is produced by a situation, for example, an intense prayer meeting. The problem here is that the powerful experience may not last; it needs to be incorporated into the ongoing steps of the spiritual life. Left to themselves, such experiences wither and die.

The call of the Gospel always demands sacrifice and change in ways described by Our Lord in His teaching, especially in the parables and the Sermon on the Mount. It demands effort in the acquisition of virtue and the rejection of vice, or bad habits. These are ways that help us to differentiate a natural religious experience from a supernatural experience of grace.

✦ **When someone experiences a radical conversion to Christ, does he experience a foretaste of heaven? Does he momentarily catch a glimpse of the unitive, or highest, way of the spiritual life?**

Often the first experiences of grace are very powerful. They are turning from darkness to light. They can have a profound emotional effect, which is not bad, but it is not the most significant part of the conversion experience, although it is what they will remember. The conversion may be very powerful and real. Saint Augustine describes it as God shining a light in his soul. People frequently say: "I am a different person," and like our Lord's words to Nicodemus, they experience being born again (see John 3:5). They have come to life. On the other hand, someone who has always led a devout life and tried to be a good Christian will, at the time of a conversion, experience an increased closeness of God's presence and a spiritual intimacy unknown before.

✦ **When some people experience a powerful conversion, they are ready to leave everything and follow Christ in a radical way. Is there a rule about whether people should make life decisions right after conversion?**

Generally speaking, people need advice and help following a conversion. They should contact an experienced spiritual director or, if that is not possible, a devout believer who has common sense. The director can help the convert to differentiate emotional experiences from the true work of grace. There are no general rules to guide people in this area. Some people make dramatic moves, which often prove disappointing; then they come to realize that they had assumed that all their own thoughts were inspired by God. It is my observation that the Holy Spirit often gets blamed for things He had little or nothing to do with. There are those, on the other hand, who fail to make any great change at a time of grace, and they revert to their state of half-faith or mediocrity. People in this situation require help and advice. For this reason, religious orders traditionally have novice masters and others who help people at the beginning of the spiritual life.

✦ **When someone experiences an awakening, or powerful conversion, it seems easy to follow Christ and perform spiritual activities of prayer and charity. Is it normal for that zeal and readiness to fade, or is it the result of our sinfulness?**

This is the experience of religious enthusiasm, which is real enough, but because it is primarily emotional, it does not last. Emotions are, of necessity, passing. Convictions of mind and will last. Some of those who had been enraptured, or mesmerized, by experiencing the Holy Spirit in the charismatic renewal may no longer even go to church; others have learned by patience the necessity of conviction, with which they have replaced emotion. In this way the Holy Sprit's work is accomplished in them with lasting effect.

✦ **You have occasionally noted that people who were terminally ill seemed to move through the stages of the spiritual life very quickly. Why is this the case and what lesson can be learned by those of us who aren't in that situation?**

My observation is that the terminally ill who surrender to God, practice faith, trust, and acceptance of His will make rapid progress on the spiritual journey. Figuratively, they seem to get on a jet plane. This happens because the great task of the spiritual life is to surrender our lives and wills to God and relinquish our hold even on the best things of this earthly life. Everyone faces the causes of death and then death itself. Those who put themselves into God's hands, accept what occurs, and use their willpower to do the best they can, accepting the treatment they may receive, seem to me to make rapid spiritual gain. I have described this in *A Priest Forever*, the life of Father Eugene Hamilton, a young seminarian who was ordained a priest in the hour of death. I believe he made tremendous spiritual progress in a very short time. Those who deal with the terminally ill who are believers may notice this. Spiritual writers have traditionally stressed that trust in God is the best form of worship.

✦ **Can we tell where we are in the spiritual life? Does the wish to know indicate that we are still at the beginning and filled with pride?**

People should try, with the help of a director or friend, to determine where they are in the spiritual life. If they are genuinely where they are supposed to be and have made some progress, that knowledge should not make them proud. The spiritual life brings with it a growing recognition that all the good we do or have comes from God by His unmerited grace. If people become even slightly preoccupied with the concept of their progress and are elated by it, they are going backwards and losing ground. Those who are making progress are growing in the knowledge that everything comes from, depends on, and returns to God. As the Lord said to Saint Catherine of Siena, "I am everything, and you are nothing." That seems harsh to a beginner, but it makes sense to those who have made some progress on the way.

IV.

THE PURGATIVE WAY

Purgative			
FIRST CONVERSION	**Moral Conversion**	**Mature Faith**	**Trust in God**
GROWTH IN VIRTUE	Moral Virtues	Faith	Hope

✦ **What is the purgative way? How does it relate to spiritual growth?**

The purgative way, as the words indicate, is a stage of purification in the spiritual life during which vices, bad habits, and egocentrism are eliminated, or greatly reduced. Vices are habitual ways of acting in the wrong way. They may be major tendencies to sin, or minor habits contrary to the very being of God, like telling white lies.

✦ **Are there stages within this stage?**

Yes, there are three major phases indicated by classical authors on the spiritual life: purgation of sin or moral integration, mature faith, and trust in God.

PRAYER FOR BEGINNERS

Since beginners are usually aware of the spiritual life by their experience of prayer, we begin with questions about prayer at this level.

✦ **What type of prayer is characteristic of the purgative way?**

Prayer experienced in the purgative way will relate largely to the particular phase the person is in. Meditation on rejecting sin and doing good is the prayer of the first phase. Mature faith leads to a more contemplative meditation on the truths of God. Simple acts of trust, in which fear and anxiety are surrendered, are typical of the third phase.

✦ **Why is prayer so important in the spiritual life?**

All people who engage in the spiritual life pray or attempt to pray, which is obviously necessary for anyone growing spiritually. We might say that prayer is the breathing of the spiritual life. It is the way the seeker is joined to the absolute, invisible, and all-holy God. Prayer is the most important way we link our lives to God. Small children usually learn to pray by reciting rote prayers, which gradually take on more meaning. Many of us learned our first prayer from an old Puritan prayer book, "Now I lay me down to sleep." Later in life prayer takes on different forms, expressing individual experiences and needs of the moment, and we will explore some of these.

✦ **Does the style of prayer change as we grow in the spiritual life?**

Since prayer reflects our side of our relationship with God, it will change and mature and indicate far more accurately than any good works where we are in relationship to Him. Some people — a chosen few — appear to have related very well to God even when they were children. If they are careful and follow the Gospel and Church teaching, they may preserve their simplicity of prayer and grow imperceptibly. This is particularly noticeable among devout unsophisticated people without much formal education. It can be very refreshing for those struggling in the spiritual life to pray, or discuss prayer, with a simple Gospel soul who is in touch with the "sweet Lord Jesus" every day. It can also be moving to pray the Rosary with those who have been doing it all their lives and still find it a mature expression of their prayer. Our Lord's words are very significant: "Blessed are the poor in spirit, for theirs is the kingdom of heaven" (Matthew 5:3).

✦ **How is prayer an indicator of where we are in the spiritual life?**

Styles of prayer, or ways of praying, are obviously linked to the different experiences that provide the focus of a particular stage in the spiritual life. One kind of prayer will be characteristic of the struggle to overcome sin. An altogether different kind of prayer will characterize someone who has entered God's presence quietly and permanently. We can often tell from these styles where someone is on the spiritual journey.

On the other hand, for those who struggle to pray while seeking to improve their lives, their style of prayer will be linked to where they are on the spiritual journey. Simply put: tell me how you pray, and I will be able to tell where you are on the road to God.

✦ **Is it possible that we may pray beyond our level of spiritual development?**

For a moment or a period of time we may experience a type of prayer that is beyond our level of development. Spiritual development is like any other human development. We often go beyond where we are for a moment. Development would not be possible if this did not occur. It is worthwhile to watch a young baby struggling to walk. Instinctively, the baby will try to stand and take a few steps and will fall down, usually in a sitting position. He may laugh or cry, but he tries again. If he did not try to walk, which for the moment is beyond his ability, he would never get to walk well. Growth always comes about in small stages and brings us a bit beyond the level to which we have been accustomed. This is as true in the life of prayer as it is in every other area of human life.

✦ What characterizes the prayer of beginners?

People who have received an awakening or a sudden enlightenment by God's grace usually have a very positive experience. It is all new to them. They feel as though they had been blind, or half alive, that something had been missing from their life. And they have found it, or it has found them. Saint Augustine prayed, "Thou didst call and cry to me and break open my deafness: and Thou didst send forth Thy beams and shine upon me and chase away my blindness." Their experience will draw them in the direction of beginning to pray. Up to that point they have said prayers as a matter of form, by rote as it were, or reverently with a congregation, but suddenly prayer is their own. It seems to them that God is reaching out to them or that they have actively sought and found Him. This is a very positive experience, but it does not last long, as a rule.

What, then, after the awakening is the prayer of those beginning the spiritual life and going through the first step of the first way, which is conversion from sin? Usually the prayer of conversion from sin is fairly emotional. It may be read out of a book, but more likely the person is struggling, feeling defeated at times, making new resolutions, and praying to God with a certain degree of desperation. Doubts also enter this kind of prayer. "Did I imagine all of this?" This prayer is sometimes referred to as wrestling with God, an image based on the account of Jacob's wrestling with an angel (Genesis 32:22–30).

✦ **What suggestions can you make for people at this level?**

First, I would suggest getting a substantial prayer book, which will contain traditional prayers that may not be familiar, like the Creed, the Rosary, and the Divine Mercy chaplet, the Hail, Holy Queen and other prayers to Our Lady and the saints. Just by reading these prayers, the beginner can gain some knowledge of the breadth, length, and depth of the spiritual life. It is best to use prayers from the Scriptures. Certain psalms are very popular, like the twenty-third ("The Lord is my Shepherd"), the fifty-first ("Have mercy on me, O God"), or Psalm 130 ("Out of the depths I cry to Thee, O Lord"). The beginner may not be prepared to understand all the psalms or use them wisely, but a few psalms in a good standard prayer book will be a good starting point. The person should think about the prayer's meaning while reading it slowly. This is the beginning of meditation.

A number of very good prayer books have been published and are frequently available in religious bookstores. I edited such a prayer book, *Prayers for Today*, by Terence Cardinal Cooke (Alba House, 1991). It includes traditional prayers and those composed by the saintly cardinal. The most important quality of prayer is constancy and fidelity. People must learn to pray even when they don't feel like it. Prayer must be recognized as the believer's duty to the Holy Trinity, our Creator, Redeemer, and Sanctifier.

UNDERSTANDING THE PURGATIVE WAY

✦ **What is the connection between the purgative way and our Lord's command that His followers "die" to themselves?**

The death of self refers not to the physical death of the person, who is God's creation and child, but to the self that has developed as a mask over that person. The mask is composed partly of the personality — the means by which our person interacts with the world outside the mind — and partly of a whole set of particular styles and ways of judging and acting that tend to favor our own importance. This is really a result of original sin. On the one hand, we must take care of and be responsible for ourselves; on the other hand, the self can be a false god, to which we relate as being of supreme importance. To be more precise, it might be best to say that it is not so easy to die to the false god of self, which Jesus calls us to do. Even our best intentions and our most devout thoughts are intertwined with the false self. That is why the process of going beyond self is called purification, or purgation.

✦ How does the purgative way relate to Church teaching on Purgatory?

The Church's teaching on Purgatory is often misunderstood, although it has deep roots in the spiritual life. Christian writers in the second century were already speaking of the soul's journey of purification after death. None of the Church Fathers thought that we save ourselves. Since the beginning of Christianity the doctrine has been recognized, as Saint Paul and others teach in the New Testament, that Christ alone is our Savior. It is also Church teaching that He requires us to live according to His teachings and to cooperate with Him in order to receive His grace of salvation. "If you love me, you will keep my commandments" (John 14:15). Those who do not do this, even though they have the grace of salvation, have not completed their task in this life. For that reason it was assumed, based on certain texts of Sacred Scripture, that a kind of journey took place after death. Unfortunately, the journey began to be seen in the Middle Ages as a prison, where people did time for their sins. While the expiatory aspect and understanding of Purgatory is not wrong, the saints who teach about Purgatory speak of it primarily as purification. Saint Augustine speaks of the purging fires after death. For ancient people fire was understood as a means of purification.

Perhaps the best understanding of Purgatory is found in the writings of the fifteenth-century mystic, Saint Catherine of Genoa.[6] This remarkable laywoman, who is credited with the beginning of the Catholic Reformation, said that the fire of Purgatory was the soul's burning desire to be purified and united with God. She taught that God stands at the open gates of heaven beckoning the soul on, but it struggles to free itself from its self-imposed impurities. Like the Church Fathers, Catherine of Genoa sees the experience of Purgatory becoming more and more positive as the soul divests itself of its stains and imperfections of will. If it were properly understood, many Christians who deny Purgatory would embrace the common sense of this teaching, which is related to several New Testament passages. It is interesting to note that because the souls in Purgatory are already saved and entering into eternal life, Purgatory is really a part of heaven, a kind of entranceway. Thus, Saint Catherine says that the happiness of the holy souls in Purgatory is exceeded only by the happiness of the saints in heaven.

✦ **The chart (see page 34) shows not only the stages of the spiritual journey and typical prayer experience but also the relationship between the decrease of anxiety-driven need and the increase of peace and freedom as the soul moves through the purgative way and into the illuminative way. Would it be true to say that what moves the soul through the purgative way is trust? Christ revealed the prayer "Jesus, I trust in you" to Saint Faustina. This single phrase sums up the whole way of purification.**

The chart on which I sum up the teachings of major spiritual writers on the three ways is not at all original. My own theory, which may be wrong, is that real spiritual progress is made through the surrender of the false self, and that leads to freedom and peace. I believe that when our level of freedom and peace has grown to the extent that it exceeds our level of anxiety and driven need, we enter the second phase of the spiritual journey, which is illumination. This is only my theory. It is certainly true that the experience of growing in trust and confidence in God, which is found in all great spiritual writings, is precisely the task as time goes on. Modern saints who speak of and illustrate trust in God include Thérèse of Lisieux, Maximilian Kolbe, Padre Pio, and Faustina Kowalska.

✦ **In our post-Christian culture, remnants of Christianity survive, but the meaning and truth of Jesus' message, which the Church continues to teach, are no longer a part of our social consciousness. How do people, following conversion, discover how to live and what to do in order to follow Christ and reject what is contrary to His message?**

The sure and certain way to follow the Christian life is to be as familiar as possible with the teachings of Christ Himself, the other teachings of the New Testament, and those of the rest of the Bible. Because there are so many remnants of Christian thought around, I think it is very wise to stick as closely as possible to the teachings of Christ Himself. This has always been the hallmark of the Christian saints. They followed Christ, listened to the word of God, and did the works of God. Whether our time needs this more than any other is an interesting question, but we certainly do need it now. The Popes have used the means of the encyclical letter, especially in modern times, to apply and underscore the Gospel teachings. These letters are filled with Scripture quotations and have names like the "Gospel of Life" and "God Is Love." Using the Scriptures and the teachings of the Popes will free us from the false ideas current today. The examples of saints in our time will do the same thing. Those who are proposed for canonization and are well on the way often bring the best message to us, not because they are better informed, but because their message is more timely. They have faced the same world we face. I have learned great things about the road to God from Mother Teresa; Cardinal Cooke; Father Solanus Casey, O.F.M. Cap.; and Father John Hardon, S.J. Who has not learned something about the spiritual life from watching and appreciating the struggles of Pope John Paul II?

Moral Integration

✦ Saint Augustine's prayer, "Convert me, Lord, but not yet," is familiar, at least in sentiment, to all who have struggled to live a moral life while feeling called to a deeper relationship with Christ. How is living a Christlike life related to the way of purgation?

We are all aware of our moral shortcomings, failures, and even our sins, although the latter are frequently covered up and denied. As we try to relate more deeply to our Lord Jesus Christ in the life of grace, we must uproot any deliberate sin. We must begin with all grave sins and continue on to the little sins or peccadilloes, like impatience, minor acts of unkindness, failure to dispel improper thoughts, and telling "white lies."

✦ Is there a point at which the struggle to overcome a particular sin indicates an addiction rather than a free decision to break the soul's relationship with God?

Addictions are pleasure-producing, irresistible compulsions, which are always self-destructive. To fulfill the definition of an addiction, the behavior must contain elements of self-destruction. For that reason, it is proper to speak of an addiction to substances like alcohol, to actions like gambling and sexual misbehavior, and many other things. It is to misuse the term somewhat to speak of a workaholic. A workaholic is a compulsive worker, but generally not destructively so. The workaholic needs to get his compulsion, not his addiction, under control. When someone finds it impossible to control immoral and self-destructive behavior, an addiction should be suspected. Strangely, addictions may show up in later life, although usually they begin in adolescence.

✦ How does addictive behavior affect spiritual growth?

Addictions affect the spiritual life in one of several ways. They may bring someone to his knees in the presence of God and cause him to admit his powerlessness over the addiction. This may lead him to go through the twelve steps, which have been popularized by Alcoholics Anonymous. Those who think they are addicted should find a twelve-step program addressed to their addiction. They should at least attend some meetings and talk to recovering addicts. This requires humility and contrition and concern for others who are similarly addicted. The AA founder formulated the twelve steps on the principles of Ignatian spirituality; he learned them from a Jesuit who assisted him and a holy nun, Sister Ignatia, called the Angel of Alcoholics Anonymous.[7] These steps are completely in line with the spiritual life. On the other hand, because addictive behaviors lead to sinful actions, they may destroy the spiritual life. Those who nurse active addictions and are still trying to lead a spiritual life are going in two directions at the same time. Chances are that if they do not join a twelve-step program, they will give up entirely their attempts at the spiritual life. Some, especially before the advent of twelve-step programs, struggled unsuccessfully, but they still managed to have a spiritual life. One such person was the English mystical poet Francis Thompson, who struggled for much of his life with an addiction to opium.

✦ What aids in the spiritual life help to overcome serious temptations?

The twelve steps may be a help here as well, even without the presence of an addiction. If an addiction is not present and different types of temptation come along, the person needs to acknowledge as clearly as possible the sources and occasions of serious temptation and get rid of them. For instance, there is a very destructive epidemic of pornography in the United States. Much of it is linked to the Internet and television. If this becomes an occasion of sin for someone who wants to grow spiritually, it should be obvious that these devices should not be easily available, especially in a private setting. Jesus says, "If your right eye causes you to sin, pluck it out and throw it away; it is better that you lose one of your members than that your whole body be thrown into hell" (Matthew 5:29). I cannot think of a better application of that text than getting rid of Internet and television.

A second tool against serious temptation is meditative prayer. By this means we can look calmly at the evil that seems attractive to us and then at the will of God. To examine the temptation in the light of the divine presence, which is always with us — Father, Son, and Holy Spirit — is extremely effective. Who can turn his back on God if he is deeply aware of the divine presence?

Third, we should look to see how a temptation involves others and hurts them. A perfect example, again, would be pornography. Someone who uses pornography participates in the destruction of another person. Those who pose for pornography do it for only one reason: cocaine. They are not even paid in money. It is well known that the drug industry and the pornography industry overlap in important and damaging ways. It is rare that sins are so private that they do not affect other people.

Fourth, the person needs to meditate on the joy of being delivered from sin, and even on the joy of repentance. This is done effectively by meditating on Psalm 51. Devotion to Christ under the title of His Sacred Heart or the Divine Mercy is also very effective, as is devotion to our Blessed Lady, who surely experienced temptations in light of our Lord's suffering on the Cross. Although she was not subject to the temptations of human weakness, like her divine Son she could experience temptations and trials. The English poet William Wordsworth referred to our Lady as "our tainted nature's solitary boast." A person might also choose a patron saint to intercede for the grace to overcome temptation. There are saints who were well-known sinners, like Saint Augustine, and those who were victims of sin, like Saint Maria Goretti. The choice of a patron saint often reminds us that we have help in our struggles from the other side of time.

✦ **Is there is a correlation between an increase of sexual temptations and the attempts to embrace the spiritual life?**

It would be difficult to say for certain. Some people find that this is the case; others do not. If there is a correlation, it is probably due to the fact that those entering the spiritual life give up a number of pleasure-oriented activities. When that happens, sexual temptations can become greater. It is an interesting fact that a very strong experience of hunger for food may increase sexual desire. Therefore, when dealing with temptation, we must be prudent in the use of penance. Self-indulgence in food can easily make us weak and subject to temptations, but too much fasting may actually increase temptations.

✦ **Our culture seems to have lost any real sense of sin, which, when acknowledged, is often psychologized or explained away as a genetic predisposition. How valid is the traditional notion of sin? How can we determine moral culpability in the struggle to overcome temptation, for instance, of a sexual nature?**

It is true that our culture has lost a sense of sin, perhaps as a result of popular psychology, which during the twentieth century was dominated by a materialistic view of human nature. Much psychological writing was at least subtly antireligious. Nonetheless, I would think that the greatest source of moral negligence and unawareness is greed and worldliness. Saint Paul says that the love of money is the root of all evil (see 1 Timothy 6:10). Our culture is extremely materialistic and consumer-oriented. Anyone interesting in pursuing the spiritual life should forgo some material advantages and comforts and use the money they thereby save for the care of the poor. Saint Vincent de Paul said that if you love the poor, your life will be filled with sunlight and you will not be frightened at the hour of death. Read the lives of the saints, who though personally frugal and abstemious, were nonetheless extremely generous with others, especially the poor and the weak.

The struggle between psychological understanding and the recognition of sin is somewhat complex. In the past there was little or no recognition that psychological wounds predisposed people to sinful behavior and therefore to some degree exonerated them from guilt. This was formally recognized in classical moral theology as four things that reduced the culpability of a sinful action, namely, ignorance, violence, fear, and concupiscence (weakness of the flesh). When best understood, modern psychological theory has explored the idea of concupiscence. Where it went wrong, it created the impression that all driven immoral behavior is to be accepted rather than simply to be understood.

On the other hand, there is a great moral laxity in the ranks of those who consider themselves good Christians or religious at the present time. This moral laxity does not stem as much from psychology as from expedient moral theology, which was very much in vogue in the 1970s and 1980s. I was teaching psychology in different seminaries at the time, and it was ironic that I was often subject to severe criticism and even dismissal for defending traditional Catholic theology while teaching counselling and psychology. At this stage of history, the John Paul II generation (roughly those between the ages of eighteen and thirty-five), which by God's Providence seems to have a much stronger commitment to morality, has made these adventures in expedient moral theology appear to be what they actually were: wrong and destructive. Unfortunately, there has been no acknowledgment on the part of those who led us astray that they went in the wrong direction. They could still do a tremendous amount of good if they were to acknowledge now that they had been wrong, even if it was with the best intentions, which was often the case. This gigantic battle between right and wrong, between virtue and sin, which took place in Catholic seminaries and institutions of higher education, is now coming to an end because of the moral values of the JP II generation. They have often tasted the bitter fruit of immoral lives and know that they were led astray.

Mature Faith

✦ **What exactly is mature faith? How do we go about growing up in our faith?**

Mature faith, as distinguished from childlike or adolescent faith, is an act of the will that accepts the mystery of God. Einstein defines a mystery as a reality, the existence of which we can know but the inner workings of which are incomprehensible to our minds. This definition, which the scientist applies to God, is helpful to keep in mind. Unfortunately, Christians of recent years tend, on the one hand, to want everything to be comprehensible and, on the other, to reject God's mysteries because they do not match what we *think* of as our scientific point of view. This tendency has taken strong hold in scholarship and affects Catholic institutions of higher learning. According to Saint John of the Cross, mature faith is a dark night to the intelligence because it reveals things we have never known either in themselves or through any kind of comparison. The most obvious example is the existence of God. We know what human existence is, we have some vague idea of what animal existence is, but we have no idea of existence above ourselves, especially infinite, absolute, unchanging, timeless existence. This is the existence in which God lives. To grow up in faith is to be able to accept the mystery of God, the mystery of the Incarnation, or God's coming among us, to confront evil and the mystery of eternal life.

The teachings of Pope Benedict XVI are a joy to those who are familiar with the theological method. He is careful, accurate, and clear. Not all theologians are like that. There is an abiding sense of faith and the reality of faith running through his writings, as there was in the writings of Pope John Paul II. Both men confronted the skepticism of modern times and have gone beyond it.

✦ Is it part of our spiritual growth to have a grave crisis of faith?

A crisis of faith is not the experience of everyone. It usually comes to people with some education who have a fair amount of academic intelligence. Many bright, intelligent, yet unsophisticated people who are competent in practical skills do not experience a crisis of faith. They are often puzzled by the difficulties of faith endured by more intellectual people. Intelligence is an amplification factor. If we do well, it makes us do better; if we do badly, it makes us do worse. That is why some of the most intelligent people occasionally say quite stupid things concerning matters of faith. This is what Saint Paul is talking about when he writes: "For the foolishness of God is wiser than men" (1 Corinthians 1:25).

✦ What other trials usually accompany the maturing of faith?

As our faith matures, we may find that expressions of faith, which were meaningful in earlier life, are no longer that significant. We need to move on. People often get stuck with what they learned as college students. They will be attracted to certain good ideas, but they need to move on. The faith of advanced contemplative people is very simple. I recall once giving a beautiful spiritual book to an old nun, Sister Mercy, a physician, who had been a contemplative religious for many years. She gave it back to me, saying, "It's too busy. I can only be quiet and pray." She had achieved a high level of maturity of faith.

The Prayer of Faith

✦ **After voluntary sin has been overcome substantially, especially serious sin but in fact all completely voluntary sin, what is prayer like in the second step of the first way, namely, the growth in mature faith?**

Most beginners are uninformed about the things of faith. This can range from those whose religious lives, perhaps as non-practicing Catholics, have been lukewarm, to those who have been either material or formal atheists. Suddenly the vast vistas of the world of faith are open before them. What does it really mean, for instance, to believe in God as an infinite being who goes beyond time and nature? What does it mean to believe in our Redeemer, who suffered and died for us? What does it mean to believe that we are motivated and directed by the life-giving Spirit of God? These are but a few of the questions related to faith, and they grow almost organically out of the prayer of beginners, who need, however, to spend more and more time directly considering the content and meaning of faith.

✦ **What does a particular truth of faith mean to everyone, and what does it mean to me?**

Many people have found it helpful to come together to pray and consider the truths of faith. This was the origin, five centuries ago, of the Oratory of Divine Love.[8] The word *oratory* means prayer group. Oratorians do just this, basing their prayer and consideration on the reading of holy Scripture. Meditations from the Oratory have begun to be published by Our Sunday Visitor, and they also appear regularly at the website *oratorydl.org.*[9] A great many contemporary spiritual movements call for weekly or monthly prayer groups, usually led by devout lay Christians.

Even if we cannot pray with others, it is essential to focus our attention on particular truths of faith. A great many solid Christian spiritual books are based on that kind of prayer experience. They may range from books of apologetics, which deal with the reasons and proofs of truths of faith, to books on the experiences of individual converts.[10]

✦ **Does the person's mind and thinking, then, become the primary focus of prayer?**

Yes, but the response of the whole being — including the heart — is always necessary. Along with learning the truths of faith, we must stand in wonder and awe at the glory of God being revealed around us. The development of a sense of God's presence and power is imperative if prayer is to continue to grow. Many people fail here because their minds are working more rapidly than their inner feelings. They learn facts about Scripture or about faith, but they do not respond interiorly to these truths.

One of the strengths of the Charismatic Renewal and of movements like Cursillo is to lead people together in total response of mind and heart to the truths of faith.

✦ **What about doubts, if they come into the prayer experience?**

Doubts can be very useful. They sharpen our perception, strengthen our arguments, and they help us to wrestle with ourselves. Doubts are by no means always a bad thing. They often reflect a new level of development, which has to be examined. The writings of many saints indicate their struggle with doubts. The experience of Saint Thérèse of Lisieux, recounted in the *Story of a Soul*, illustrates the point well. Her doubts had their origin in the extreme depression that was part of the symptoms of tuberculosis. She expresses them in her autobiography, giving courage and strength to many others in times of doubt.

✦ **Can doubts be the work of Satan?**

Yes, but on different occasions in the spiritual life we have the opportunity to confront and contradict the Prince of Darkness. Satan gives us the opportunity to struggle and fight for the truth of God. A marvelous image, often found in medieval cathedral windows, shows a snarling dog twisted around to bite its own tail. This is a humorous depiction of Satan, who by the grace of God often defeats himself when attempting to entrap human souls. It is good to remember this, since sooner or later everyone encounters the negative influences of the Prince of Darkness.

THE BIBLE AND THE SPIRITUAL LIFE

✦ **What is the place of Scripture in this struggle and in all aspects of the spiritual life?**

Anyone operating on the level of faith should take the time to become familiar with the whole Bible, its content, divisions, and many books. Any number of books are available at present to assist people to learn about the Bible. This is no small task. A good Catholic bookstore can be an invaluable aid in finding books that will instruct and help us to understand the whole Bible and its meaning. There is no need to hurry along in biblical study. Take your time and do it well.

Once you have a general grasp of the Bible, and have perhaps taken an introductory course on Sacred Scripture, you should begin to savor particular books that are meaningful and appealing. Of preeminent importance are the Gospels; then the other New Testament books, which constitute a commentary on the Gospels. It should be pointed out that some books, like the epistle to the Romans, are initially difficult to read and comprehend. Some guidance is usually necessary when we take on the writings of Saint Paul, whereas the Gospels, which are even more profound, are more easily read and grasped.

A word of caution needs to be said about courses of biblical study. In secular colleges and even, sad to say, in some so-called Catholic institutions of higher learning some approaches to these studies are riddled with skepticism. This has been going on for several decades and has undermined the faith of many, particularly the vitality of religious communities, which were based on the observance of the Gospel. Be extremely careful of taking a course with a title like "The Bible as Literature." Even other courses may be founded on skeptical or ill-advised theories. Some of the theories may have some validity, but beginners in the spiritual life are usually not prepared to deal with the intricacies and subtleties of such approaches. It is worthwhile to remember that there are canonized saints who never even read the Bible, because they did not know how to read. They heard its message in sermons and saw its glories in stained-glass windows, and they knew the word of the Lord. On the other hand, there are people today who, calling themselves biblical scholars, are avowed atheists and agnostics. This is an area where caution must be exercised. One current writer who is especially cautious about biblical theories is Pope Benedict XVI. His book *Jesus of Nazareth* would provide an excellent introduction to biblical studies for many readers.[11]

One work I have found immensely helpful in developing a real relationship with Christ is Msgr. Romano Guardini's *The Lord*.[12]

Several approaches to the biblical studies are possible. Some are called "critical" approaches, which does not mean that the writer wishes to criticize the word of God. They attempt rather to give it meaning with contemporary language and ideas. We do not need a great understanding of these various methods, most of which are speculation, in order to read Sacred Scripture intelligently and spiritually. On the other hand, commentaries on the Scriptures by the Church Fathers are extremely valuable.

✦ What is the Liturgy of the Hours?

This is the term often used to describe the "prayer book" of the Church. It has grown out of the Church's monastic and religious offices over many centuries. In the not-so-distant past it was called the "Divine Office" because it was understood as the important office, or duty, of all priests and many religious to a certain form of prayer, or divine service, to God. Although it forms part of the Church's liturgy, it is separate and distinct from the Mass and administration of the sacraments. It is organized around the recitation of the psalms, Scripture readings, hymns, and sermons by the Church Fathers and Doctors at specific times of the day and night. It is a good idea to work one's way gradually into the Liturgy of the Hours, possibly by obtaining a small book that contains only Morning Prayer, Evening Prayer, and Night Prayer. Several editions are available in Catholic bookstores. The next step is to graduate to the four-volume series, which includes the Office of Readings and prayers to be said during the daytime hours. The Office of Readings changes each day, and over a year's time it provides a good selection of long biblical passages and commentaries by the Fathers and Doctors of the Church. The most popular of all commentaries are by Saint Augustine, which are used for more than eighty readings.

✦ Is there a danger in trying to do too much in the spiritual life?

It is important at this time to watch out for spiritual gluttony. Enthusiasm can bring with it the temptation to try to live the life of a contemplative monk or nun. No less an authority than Saint Francis de Sales warns us about this in his *Introduction to the Devout Life*. This is a very worthwhile book to read at this point in the spiritual life. Since the seventeenth century it has been an immensely popular work not only with Catholics but also with Protestants, despite the fact that in his day many were extremely hostile to the old faith. His writings are very revealing to anyone beginning the spiritual life.

✦ **Is there a good guide to the Catholic faith for those moving through this age of the spiritual life so that their prayer may reflect the truths of faith?**

A perfect guide is the *Catechism of the Catholic Church* and solid commentaries on it.[13] The *Catechism* was published with the great encouragement of Pope John Paul II and under the direction of Christoph Cardinal Schönborn, archbishop of Vienna, who is vitally involved in the spiritual life. The *Catechism* is a theological treasure house, written from the viewpoint of faith. Catholics at the present time cannot consider themselves to have a well-rounded spiritual life unless they are familiar with the *Catechism*. It is not a book that is normally read cover to cover, nor can it be used simply as a prayer book. Instead, one reads articles and sections of particular importance in order to have a grasp of the subject presented, for instance, the Incarnation and the Church's moral teachings. From there it is a small step to making meditations on the truths of faith.

✦ **What is meant by the mystery of faith? How does it apply at this juncture of the spiritual life?**

The word "mystery" leaves many people puzzled. Albert Einstein, who had a profound sense of mystery, described a mystery as a truth whose existence we can perceive but whose inner workings are incomprehensible to our limited minds. That definition applies not only to natural mysteries like the nature of gravity, time, and biological life but also to supernatural mysteries. The difference is that some supernatural mysteries like the Holy Trinity are absolutely incomprehensible.

✦ **If these truths are incomprehensible, how can we deal with them?**

The answer is by prayerful meditation. Supernatural mysteries can be grasped only with the words of divine revelation. We can make assertions based on divine revelation — for instance, that there are three persons in God — but we don't comprehend in any full sense what a divine person is. We scarcely understand what a human person is. Still less do we understand celestial citizens, whom we call angels; they too are persons. Just sit for a moment and think what it must be like to be a pet, a friendly dog, which is not a person but can be said to possess something like a personality. If even animals are mysteries to us, surely beings who are above us are far greater mysteries and ultimately incomprehensible.

It is by prayer that the depths of mystery can enter our lives. It was Einstein's opinion that those who look at the natural mysteries of the physical world without reverence and awe might as well be dead.

> The most beautiful and most profound emotion we can experience is the sensation of the mystical. It is the sower of all true science. He to whom this emotion is a stranger, who can no longer wonder and stand rapt in awe, is as good as dead. To know that what is impenetrable to us really exists, manifesting itself as the highest wisdom and the most radiant beauty which our dull faculties can comprehend only in their most primitive forms — this knowledge, this feeling is at the center of true religiousness.[14]

What about the Christian, even a theologian, who writes and speaks about the mysteries of faith without a profound sense of reverence and prayer? Such a person can make religion the dullest subject in the world. This is why a life of prayer is essential for mature faith.

A prayerful appreciation of mystery is extremely important for those who are trying to grow in mature faith. They should feel drawn into what is known as the "obedience of faith." We must kneel before God in His absolute, mysterious nature and accept what He has revealed to us. We experience this when we immerse ourselves in the words of Sacred Scripture, especially in the words of Christ. We are also guided by the Church's traditional teaching because Christ has promised to teach the Church all things, and He has sent the Holy Spirit to guide us that we may know all truth (see, for example, John 14:16–17; 26).

All Christians should belong to a devout, prayerful community that is guided by both tradition and Scripture. Tradition does not have quite the same force as Scripture, but it guides us in the proper interpretation of Scripture and helps us avoid erroneous private interpretations. The following Scripture text is an invaluable help to memorize at this stage of the spiritual life:

> O the depth of the riches and wisdom and knowledge of God! How unsearchable are his judgments and how inscrutable his ways! "For who has known the mind of the Lord, or who has been his counselor?" "Or who has given a gift to him that he might be repaid?" For from him and through him and to him are all things. To him be glory for ever. Amen. (Romans 11:33–36)

✦ **Is the failure to have a sense of and appreciation for mystery part of the present confusion in Christianity?**

Yes. It seems to me that this is much of our current problem. Many, including teachers and writers of theology, do not have a grasp of what it means to have the "obedience of the faith." Scripture speaks of this obedience directly and through many examples. Read, for instance, the opening of the epistle to the Romans, where Saint Paul speaks of "Jesus Christ our Lord, through whom we have received grace and apostleship to bring about the obedience of faith for the sake of his name among all the nations" (Romans 1:4–5).

Modern people are programmed to evaluate everything according to their own experiences and estimations. This is not necessarily a bad thing, and much of democracy rests and depends on such an approach. However, it leaves people unprepared for the obedience of faith. Modern people who wish to be fervent Christians have to make a clear distinction between opinions — whether they be personal, popular, or accurate — and the truths of faith and the obedience owed to them. Obedience to faith is often paid mere lip service, but when people begin to speculate, especially if motivated by outside influences, they lose the sense of mystery that is necessary to grow in mature faith. The antidote to all this is a serious personal commitment to a life of prayer.

✦ Do doubts indicate a lack of mature faith?

Doubts can certainly be a sign of a lack of mature faith and of understanding of the "obedience of faith." Faith, after all, means several different things. It is an act by which we tell God and ourselves that we accept the truths He has revealed. Faith is also a gift, or grace. We could not have true faith unless we had received the grace of faith. We sometimes meet people who do not have faith, although they may have positive attitudes toward religion. The grace of faith has not been given them, and they should be encouraged to pursue the truths of faith. Many Christians like Saint Augustine went through the experience of being drawn to faith before they actively accepted the gift.

Doubts can arise from ideas current in the world around us that are not integrated into the world vision of faith. Faith brings with it a certain way of looking at things, first at the world around us and then at God and ourselves. Science and the scientific point of view are frequently misused to challenge faith. People who understand the nature of science and have some comprehension of the nature of religious faith know that properly understood, neither can contradict the other. Science is about the measurable, the tangible, what we experience with our senses. Faith by its very nature is about what goes beyond our senses. We can perceive many things in the world that lead us to desire faith or to make an act of faith, like a starry sky that preaches the power and infinity of the Creator. A misunderstanding of science, however, may provide people with reasons for not accepting faith. I am convinced that such reasons are fundamentally invalid. If they are properly understood, the two realms of faith and science are quite distinct. But while they are quite distinct, they are in many ways quite compatible and they complement one another because of the ultimate unity of truth. I have tried to explore this in my book *Why Do We Believe?*[15]

✦ Is it true that faith could lead to obscure and odd ideas?

True and mature faith will not do this. The practice of the virtue of the gift of faith will not lead anyone astray. However, along with faith, we have opinions. We often do not distinguish our religious opinions from what we believe by faith. People have opinions, for example, about whether Mass should be offered in the vernacular languages or only in Latin. That question pertains to the practice of religion in general or to its practice for the individual. It does not pertain directly to faith. In fact, there is no indication that Our Lord ever said a word in Latin, but it is an ancient usage, which in the course of time became the vehicle for the communication of Scripture and liturgy in Western Europe. Whether people accept or reject the use of the vernacular languages in liturgy, they may see the debate in terms of their faith, but it is not a question pertinent to faith. There are many views and questions like this in popular discussions today.

✦ **Is it safe to say that those who are trying to live a life of faith should believe and accept everything they have heard in church or from religious teachers?**

Emphatically no. There was a time long ago, when I was growing up, that whatever was heard at Mass or in a religious education program would mostly likely conform to Church teaching. Unfortunately, in the latter part of the twentieth century this was no longer true. People must, therefore, be discriminating. One of the reasons that led Pope John II to have a new Catechism published was precisely in order that Catholic people would have available to them a clear statement of the Catholic faith even in its finer points. Unfortunately, it has been my experience that people can hear things from the pulpit or in the classroom that are at least at odds with common Catholic teaching and, sadly, sometimes completely heretical. I know several people who have encountered extreme spiritual problems and dangers, even coming to a loss of faith, because of teachings that are based almost entirely on human speculation and estimation. Faith reveals, as Saint John of the Cross tells us, things that we have neither seen nor known, either as they are in themselves or by any comparison. He says that for this reason faith appears as darkness for the individual, a darkness that occurs because of the brightness of its light. This is one of the reasons that meditative prayer that integrates the teachings of faith into our inmost consciousness is essential.

The English poet John Dryden put this very well when he wrote:

> *Thy throne is darkness in th' abyss of light,*
> *A blaze of glory that forbids the sight.*
> *O teach me to believe Thee thus conceal'd,*
> *And search no farther than Thyself reveal'd.*[16]

His contemporaries in the Holy Land thought they knew Jesus of Nazareth. This was true of both His enemies and His apostles. Only after the Resurrection did human beings begin to have some dim awareness that they were dealing with the only-begotten Son of God. This belief is still what Pope Benedict XVI calls the "scandal of Christianity"; it goes completely beyond human comprehension. The complete and faithful acceptance of Christ's divinity is essential if we are to make spiritual progress as a Christian. A non-Christian who has not been given the gift of faith can make progress, but a Christian who literally cheats the gift of faith will end up in the spiritual doldrums.

✦ **How do we work to increase our faith?**

Christ Himself says the simple rule is to follow Him. He is the Way. There are many aspects to growing in faith: reading the Gospels, the other books of Sacred Scripture and the writings of the Church Fathers; understanding the application of the faith at the present time, defending and explaining the faith to others, and practicing the faith through works of devotion and adoration. God's greatest gift to Catholics today is probably devotion to the presence of Christ in the Holy Eucharist. This is specifically a Catholic devotion, largely attributable to Saint Francis of Assisi. It is a great act of faith, and it is Christian prayer in the best sense.

An interesting and ironic turn in modern history can be seen in the life of Albert Einstein. Arguably, one of the greatest scientists who ever lived, Einstein had a profound sense of mystery, as we have indicated. Although he apparently did not come to accept the God of revelation, he was fascinated by the Catholic teaching of the Holy Eucharist. I knew this from several independent sources. It is interesting to compare this with the attitudes of some Catholics, including some clergy and teachers, who directly or indirectly disparage the mysterious meaning of the Eucharist. It is my hope that the practice of faith among Catholics will return to greater strength in the immediate future by reason of prayerful devotion to Christ's presence in the Eucharist. There we confront the mystery of faith.

Trust

✦ **What is the role of "giving thanks in all circumstances," as Saint Paul advises? How does that help our trust in God to mature?**

The problem of evil includes physical evil, like sickness, and moral evil, like the wicked deeds of men. It also involves something in between, namely, the wicked deeds of men caused by the circumstances in which they function and because of which they have perhaps less responsibility — for instance, the situation of a person born and raised in a criminal environment. All these things bring with them suffering, sorrow, and sometimes catastrophe. It has been the secret of the saints, following Christ's example, to accept evil and do the best with it that they can. Naturally, we should try to undo evil before its effects occur, as we do with medicine and attempts to avoid war or harmful human circumstances. When all else fails and evil is upon us, we have to trust that God will bring good out of evil. This is the message of Christ's holy life. Out of the worst evil ever done by men, the worst sin ever committed, Christ's sacrificial love and obedience brought eternal salvation and the Resurrection with the promise of eternal life.

✦ **How do we take our spiritual growth seriously without its becoming a narcissistic exercise?**

The answer to this question is the practice of humility. We must return continually to the truth that any good we have comes from God. This is true of any lasting supernatural good. Someone might feel good about himself because he can cook, but even this is a gift of God through nature. If someone does good in the name of God and is able to follow the divine law in order to grow spiritually, that is obviously a complete work of God.

✦ **In *Spiritual Passages* you mention that we can experience darkness in the purgative way. What is this experience like, and what is the best way to deal with it?**

A good deal of joy, fulfillment, and a sense of purpose in life usually characterize the purgative way. This results from the person's having escaped the trivialities of a worldly culture and having overcome the habit of simply seeking sensual pleasure. It is a positive experience and has been written of often. The joy of repentance is beautifully described in Psalm 51. Those in the purgative way may come to a moment, however, when they will miss their old self-indulgences. This reminds us of the complaints of the Israelites wandering in the desert of Sinai, wanting to go back to the cucumbers and melons of Egypt. Those who experience the pain of purgation may find that their prayer life will seem dry, and they will be tempted to go back. This is an important junction in the spiritual life. It means that faith in God is based not simply on enjoying things, however spiritual they may be.

✦ **How can we tell whether this experience indicates progress or regression in the spiritual life?**

If we are growing in trust — in the sense of confidence in God, no matter what else is going on in life — there can be little doubt that we are making progress. It is not easy to do this, because we must surrender our apparent right to feel anxious, depressed, and sorrowful about things. We often enjoy exercising this right, but by means of trust in God, we have to give up the self-indulgence of worry and fear. In psychology it is often observed that people choose to be miserable or anxious. Paradoxically, they fear the possibility of really being at peace.

✦ **How do the Beatitudes help us to grow in trust of God despite what we may feel or experience?**

The Beatitudes are mysterious statements of blessing given by our Lord in the fifth chapter of Saint Matthew's Gospel, at the beginning of the Sermon on the Mount. Spiritual writers in the past have pointed out that these remarkable blessings seem to have an almost sacramental character of their own. They are the road to infused virtues, that is, virtues that come from the Holy Spirit. They strengthen us in making progress toward God and help us to do what we would not otherwise be able to do. They are examples of infused Christian virtues rather than simple moral virtues. For example, the moral virtue of courage will help us to endure hardship and danger for some natural good, like defending the country. A supernatural Christian virtue enables us to endure difficulties and mortal danger in order to enter the kingdom of heaven or to help others to get there. These two kinds of virtue can operate at the same time.

THE PRAYER OF HOPE

✦ **What is prayer like in the third stage of the purgative way?**

We have seen that the third and last step of the first way of the interior life is trust in God. It is my impression that it may take only a few years to come to mature faith, but it may take most people a lifetime to really trust God. Many well-intentioned believers get this far, but do not go beyond this step.

Trust in God means turning over to Him everything we possess, value, and appreciate, even what we cherish the most. This is not easy to do, which is why our Lord Jesus Christ exhorted His listeners so often (and us) to trust God. In Scriptural language trust means to have faith. As we use it here, faith has a somewhat different meaning from belief in the divine mysteries — in God and in His revealed truth. Here we speak of faith in God as trust in Him and in His Providence. The word in our language that most accurately conveys the meaning of this experience is hope. Someone has said that hope is faith that has come to blossom and flower. It is hope and trust in God that makes faith truly a part of our lives and desires, but the prayer of faith and that of hope are different in several ways. We often express acts of trust or hope in God by prayers of intercession, particularly at times of tragedy or great need, asking Him to do things.

✦ **Since this type of prayer is an important part of the spiritual life, what can we learn to help us grow while we are in need and anxiety?**

This question is extremely revealing. A good many people spend much of their prayer time expressing to God their fears and concerns, or in asking that in His providential care He give them assistance or relief with serious problems. This is certainly not inappropriate. In the Gospel we see countless numbers of people coming to Our Lord with serious problems. They all ask for divine help by miracles of healing or deliverance. They sometimes express great trust in His powers, and He rewards them. He often says, "Your faith has saved you."

Even though prayers of intercession represent a less contemplative form of prayer, it seems to me it would be wise to include them as a significant part of our prayer life so long as we pray in a way that expresses faith and trust.

✦ **How is faith and trust expressed in a moment of great need or anxiety?**

The answer is, quite simply, to come into the presence of God, especially into Christ's presence, using our imaginative abilities to see His face before us and to express fervently and trustingly our trust in His assistance in a difficult situation. It is not wise or helpful to tell God what to do. We must always remember that He is not only all-powerful but also all-knowing and wise.

Believers must be prepared to accept that their petitions will not always be answered in the way they think best. It is wise not to try to tie God's hands. Christ said, "Ask, and you shall receive." He did not say, "Ask, and you shall receive the answer you think is best."

When someone we know is in danger of death from sickness or accident, we may in our anxiety pray with justification that God will spare the person. We may even ask for a miracle. At a time like this, however, we have to step back a bit and realize that God may be calling the ill or injured person home to Himself. We should try to formulate our prayer in a way that takes into account God's will. We may certainly ask that, if it is His will, death may be avoided. If, however, it is time for that person to leave this "valley of tears," this temporary life, we should pray that the person will die well "in the Lord" and with every spiritual benefit for salvation.

I speak of this prayer with some specific personal knowledge. After I had been struck by a car a few years ago, I hovered for days between life and death. It seemed to many medical professionals that there was no possibility of recovery. It also seemed that if I did survive, I would be greatly impaired. Friends with me prayed incessantly for my recovery. Thousands of people e-mailed my community that they were praying for me. Their prayers were heard, and I literally came back from the edge of death. But suppose I had died? Would that have meant that their prayers had not been heard? By no means. They would have been praying that I had a safe passage from this world to the next.

I am able to be deeply grateful now for the prayers said for me, but I hope I would have been equally grateful if they had brought me safely through the doors of death to the other side.

Many people who read these pages will remain uneasy. They will have prayed for good things that they never received. This is really where we can practice the virtue of hope. We have only to think of the Blessed Mother, who in her immense sorrow must have said many prayers when her Son was arrested, tortured, and led to death by a horrible barbaric procedure that was well known in the Holy Land at that time. There is a relentlessness to Christ's sufferings, as each event of the horrible drama unfolds, altogether in keeping with Roman legal proceedings of the period.

✦ **Did Our Lady's prayers go unanswered?**

By no means. But they were answered in a way that went beyond the comprehension of any observer. Whether Christ's Mother knew that the Resurrection would take place remains a question. Christ had spoken of His Resurrection. I think it is a safe assumption that she would have remembered His words, but nonetheless, she is venerated wisely in the Western Church as Our Lady of Sorrows and in the Eastern Church as Mother of God, Joy of All who Sorrow.

✦ **It sounds like you are saying that the prayer of trust and hope in God is an important part of the spiritual life.**

I cannot emphasize this enough. Much continues to be written about the first two steps of the spiritual life: moral conversion and the intellectual assent of faith. Not enough attention is given to the prayers of those who are desperate or in great need. This is thought of as a by-product of faith. By no means. It is the highest expression of faith. Christ says often, "Your faith has saved you."

✦ **How do we make an act of trust?**

The first thing to be done is to understand how we pray best as individuals. We may pray best with a book of fervent prayers written by others in times of great need. Many books have prayers for specific occasions like economic or family needs, illness (whether temporary or fatal), and death.

In addition, the liturgy often has beautiful prayers expressing general or special needs, which can be used for meditation for personal prayer when we are in need.

Another form of prayer of intercession or petition is what springs naturally and spontaneously from the heart. Our most fervent and attentive prayer will probably be said in times of intense need. For instance, when we are endeavoring to make advances in contemplative prayer and are beset by distractions, or when we have a flat tire in the midst of a snowstorm, we are likely to pray with absolute attention. Therefore, we should never overlook prayers of petition. In them we accept the mystery of God's Providence, the mystery of the interaction of good and evil in this life, and we express our faith in God's goodness. Think of the prayers of people in the Old Testament who were falling under the sword of their persecutors. Think of the prayers of the Christians as they went into the amphitheatre; of people as they went into the gas chambers of the concentration camps; of Saints Maximilian Kolbe and Teresa Benedicta of the Cross (Edith Stein) as they went to their deaths. Their example of trust will help you formulate your own prayers.

✦ What can we do to sustain our state of prayer during a busy day when we cannot pray formally?

The Catholic Church has always encouraged people to make aspirations — short prayers they offer during the day. It may be helpful to select a few of these. In recent years the short prayer of Saint Faustina has been very popular: "Jesus, I trust in You." These few words succinctly focus our hearts and minds on trust in God. We should also think of the Rosary, which has the ability to calm fears and focus the mind. Innumerable Rosaries have been said by those in difficult and trying circumstances. Many good Christian souls have died with the Rosary in hand, their lips moving in prayer as they passed from this world to the next.

✦ **Could it be that this kind of prayer is an obstacle to the spiritual life?**

If someone sees intercessory prayer as a way to dictate to God, there is no doubt that this prayer will keep them at an intermediate stage and they will not attain complete trust in God. However, this kind of prayer can assist someone going through great trials who has perhaps not placed everything in God's hands but is trying to do so. Repetition of prayers of trust based on the prayer, "Thy will be done on earth as it is in heaven" . . . can lead someone to great trust even if it is said with much difficulty. I recently heard of a priest falsely accused and condemned who found it almost impossible to say this phrase in the Lord's Prayer. When he could finally say it, it would be an expression of complete trust in and surrender to God. This prayer is an image of the prayer Christ said in the Garden of Gethsemane, "Not my will, but Your will, be done."

V.

THE ILLUMINATIVE WAY

Illuminative			
ENLIGHTEN-MENT	**First Darkness**	**Charity to Neighbor**	**Love of God**
GROWTH IN THEOLOGICAL VIRTUE	Strengthening of Virtue	Zeal, Kindness, Generosity, Forgiveness	Dedication, Sacrifice, Contemplative Meditation

✦ **What is the illuminative way? How does it relate to spiritual growth?**

The illuminative way is the center, or middle passage, of the journey of the three ways. It is probably the most positive experience of the three because the unitive way, which is very close to God, can also have periods of great darkness. Those in the illuminative way very much feel the light of God in their souls.

✦ **Are there stages within the illuminative way? What about the prayer of those in the illuminative way?**

Instead of stages I would rather speak of two areas of emphasis. The illuminative way is the way of the virtue of charity, just as the purgative way is the way of moral virtue, faith, and hope. The two areas of emphasis in the illuminative way are love of neighbor and love of God. They are certainly not mutually exclusive. It is noticeable that those in the illuminative way become proficient at love of neighbor and then move on to a quiet contemplative love of God. The prayer of the illuminative way is characterized by increasing quiet because the virtue of trust, which has been acquired with the virtue of hope at the end of the purgative way, now takes over. Those in the illuminative way worry far less and are less driven in what they do. They have a good perspective on the importance of things as they relate to eternal life. Consequently, they will practice the prayer known as contemplative meditation, which is often linked with a quiet and prayerful reading of the Scriptures or some other inspiring book. They will take a great deal of time and will find that just a few lines or sentences will keep them going in quiet prayer for a long time. The prayer of the illuminative way is filled with calm and quiet.

✦ **Many saints considered themselves the greatest sinners. Was that the result of piety and humility, or of a greater awareness of the true nature of sin and many personal failings?**

As people make progress toward God, it becomes obvious to them that they have been real sinners and their past sins take on an almost frightening aspect. They know a great deal more about God than they used to, and they ask themselves: How could I ever have done what I did? How could I ever have rejected God in such a way? At the same time, those in the illuminative way continue to grow in hope and trust. Their anxiety about previous sins, therefore, can become an occasion of great trust. This is all something of a paradox.

✦ **Does the struggle against sin lessen or increase as we progress on the spiritual path?**

This is a complex question. The struggle against serious and grave sin obviously lessens, because temptation and desires in that direction lessen as we make progress in the spiritual life. "[W]hat fellowship has light with darkness?" (2 Corinthians

6:14). On the other hand, we become much more aware of sin and sensitive to how it may offend God and damage our spiritual life. Sins that once seemed very minor, or of which we were not aware, may suddenly preoccupy us in the struggle to avoid sin. It is difficult to say whether this is a greater or lesser struggle. It might be compared to the difficulty of walking along a relatively flat plain, a slightly ascending and long plain, as is the purgative way, or when we are beginning to ascend the mountain where the traveling is arduous and progress seems to slow down.

✦ **What kind of prayer will come naturally to those in the illuminative way?**

Prayer in the illuminative way will naturally be a quiet, silent meditation, an awareness of God's presence. Those in the illuminative way must exercise care because they will still have obligations and needs for other kinds of prayer, especially liturgical prayer. However, their approach to liturgical prayer will be filled with greater reverence and awe. They will be far more attracted to liturgy that is quiet and prayerful than to one that is noisy and musically unnerving. Silence is an important part of the prayer of the illuminative way. They will have to make a special effort either to transform their devotions or keep them in spite of themselves. For instance, the Rosary may have been very significant to someone in the purgative way; those in the illuminative way must learn to say it in a different way, that is, with much less emphasis on the words or even on the mysteries, which are not an integral part of the Rosary. The mysteries were added by Saint Peter Canisius (1521–1597) and by Pope John Paul II. However, there are techniques that will be helpful for those making the recitation of the Rosary a sort of place where we meet God. The word *Rosary* suggests a rose garden or a circle of roses. Msgr. Guardini refers to it as a place. The Rosary was a very important part of the life of Mother Teresa.

✦ **Is someone in the illuminative way more likely to sense God's presence in the world and encounter Him in all that happens, or will such a person be more apt to try to find God in all things by individual effort?**

It is almost part of the definition of the illuminative way to have a growing sense of God's presence and, with little effort, to see His presence in many things. That is one of the most obvious traits of those at this stage of the spiritual journey. They interpret events and encounter the things of life in a prayerful, devout way — perhaps not all the time because of the press of duties and the nature of events. When we witness a fatal accident — regardless of where we may be on the spiritual journey — we will react with compassion and alarm and try to bring assistance to those who may have survived and who have to deal with the devastation around them. I don't think there is a particularly illuminative way to handle an earthquake. The illusion that those in the illuminative go through life with a knowing smile on their faces is largely a Hollywood invention. Many people I have known in the illuminative way have been great realists.

✦ **Would Mary Magdalen be a patron of those in the illuminative way, as she searched for Christ at the empty tomb when He seemed not to be there?**

Mary Magdalen has often been taken as a model for people in the spiritual life, especially those whose early lives were sinful, or not particularly devout. She was immensely popular in the Middle Ages, especially in France. Her status as a model for the spiritual life is frequently combined with Mary of Bethany. They appear to be two different people because Magdala is in Galilee, whereas Bethany is just outside Jerusalem. Taken together, the two Marys provide an interesting picture: on the one hand, we have the prayerful person who let her sister do the dishes while she listened to Christ; on the other hand, we have the penitent woman weeping at the tomb. The Magdalen may not be everyone's model, but she certainly is a beautiful illustration of how God's grace can work in the soul of someone who was in the wrong place. After all, it is said that Christ cast seven devils out of her.

✦ **What prayer characterizes the transition from the purgative to the illuminative way?**

By this time the person has learned to pray silently during the busy day, lifting the mind and heart to God. However, the transition from the purgative to the illuminative way may be for many people a time of darkness and trial. Spiritual writers have often seen this as providential, but there may also be a psychological explanation here. Periods of transition in human life, even the natural unfolding of human life, can be trying. Think of adolescence or the entrance into old age. Things we have been familiar with seem to fall away. New experiences take their place, which we may not be comfortable with. People should be prepared, therefore, for a time of difficulty and darkness as they pass from one stage to another, as at the beginning of the illuminative way. Having surrendered everything to God, they may feel at sea for a while, with nothing to hold on to. They should rely on prayer; if they cannot do anything else, they should use the psalms, the Rosary, or prayers from a prayer book to keep themselves in a prayerful attitude. Otherwise, they may lose some of the gains they have made. The meditative reading of Scripture (known as *lectio divina*), especially the Gospels, is a very helpful form of prayer.

✦ **Is it true that the illuminative way, as the term suggests, is a bright and pleasant part of the spiritual life?**

It certainly is true that the illuminative way is a brighter experience than the struggles of the purgative way, but at the same time it includes its own struggles and trials. The illuminative way means a time when the person's inner life is brightened by divine

gifts. This includes the virtue of charity towards others and especially toward God. It also includes an increase in the gifts of the
Holy Spirit, particularly wisdom and understanding. Along with
these gifts, which operate only with our moderate cooperation,
however, there are struggles and challenges, as in any other way
of life. It would be a mistake to think of the illuminative way as
a spiritual vacation.

✦ **It sounds as though God does all the work in the illuminative way.**

The soul in the illuminative way experiences the Holy Spirit's activity in a most unusual way. Forgiveness of one's enemies, for example, comes with greater ease because of the theological virtue of
charity. Prayer is generally easier and more contemplative, and
because of the gift of love of God, which is part of the virtue of charity, the person enjoys simply sitting and enjoying God's presence.

The person is also drawn by the gift of understanding, which
makes it possible to put the things of this life in proper perspective in relation to God and to see the interconnection between
various truths of faith, which may not have been obvious before.
Part of the joy of the illuminative way comes with the ability to
contemplate the meaning of the mysteries of the Christian faith:
the Incarnation, Christ's holy life, His miracles, His preaching,
and His terrible but saving death.

✦ **What are some of the struggles of the illuminative way?**

The illuminative way begins with the second conversion. Nothing in the spiritual life is free. Each step even as a gift from God
brings us to a greater level of sacrifice and consecration.

The Second Conversion
Almost all spiritual writers, including Saint John of the
Cross, indicate that there must be a second conversion. The sev-

enteenth-century Jesuit, Father Louis Lallemant, states on this subject:

> Two conversions ordinarily occur in the majority of the saints and in religious who become perfect: one, by which they devote themselves to the service of God; the other, by which they give themselves entirely to perfection. We see this fact in the lives of the apostles when Christ called them and when he sent the Holy Ghost upon them.[17]

After struggling to observe the Gospel and avoid any kind of voluntary sin, those in the illuminative way will begin, in the light of charity, to become aware of their ambition, self-centeredness, egotism, narcissism, and self-love. They also become aware of their negligence, sloth, and hypocrisy. All of this is a devastating revelation to those who thought they had been leading an interior life. It is part of the strange paradox that as we get closer to God, we realize more and more how far we are from His holiness and perfection. Those who wish to grow in the interior life must not miss the second conversion. The following quotation from Father Lallemant is most revealing:

> The Holy Ghost waits some time for them to enter into their interior and, seeing there the operations of grace and those of nature, to be disposed to follow His direction; but if they misuse the time and favor which He offers them, He finally abandons them to themselves and leaves them in their interior darkness and ignorance, which they preferred and in which they live hereafter amid great dangers for their salvation.[18]

✦ **Does this mean that the person who does not pass through the second conversion and uproot as much self-concern and egotism as possible is really in spiritual danger?**

Yes. At one time I did not realize that that was the case. At the present time in the Church, however, one sees many people, often clergy and religious, who once made serious attempts to grow in the spiritual life but who seem to have lost their way amid the confusion and worldliness of recent decades. They were once spiritual people, but they have regressed pitiably to a situation of severe mediocrity. I would be remiss not to point this out to people and to suggest strongly that they get moving and get back on track. Saint John of the Cross makes the point that those at this stage of the spiritual life who fail to struggle with the second conversion go around excusing themselves rather than changing themselves. They take pleasure in telling others of their own good qualities. This also leads, according to the Mystical Doctor, to a kind of pharisaical hypocrisy. They spend a good deal of time criticizing others and posturing as if they have made a good deal of progress, which is an illusion.

✦ **Does the Holy Spirit give any special help at this time?**

Yes. There is an experience called the passive purification of the senses. There are certain signs that this state has begun, and they are described by Saint John of the Cross.[19] The first sign, or indication, is that we find no comfort in the things of God or in created things. It may well be that this sign corresponds to what we would call depression, but it is uniquely related to this stage of the interior life. It is often difficult to distinguish one from the other, and it may not even be helpful to try.

The second sign manifested is a painful anxiety which arises because the person thinks he or she is not serving God but rather is going backwards and can sense no sweetness in the interior life. This causes dryness, and the person feels parched and empty.

Many people give up the pursuit of the spiritual life at this point. It would be helpful for people at this level to remain quiet.

The third sign of passive purification is the inability to meditate or make reflections or contemplation. Up to this point the soul has rejoiced that the thirst for God has been fed by the knowledge of God and of His presence. At this stage the person must go on, but without that sweetness and the experience of his thirst being quenched by God. This is the time when fidelity is tested, and it is important to remain faithful. We are advised to keep in mind the saying: "The roots of knowledge are bitter and the fruits sweet." We are sustained by the hope and expectation that the purification will lead us to genuine contemplative prayer.

Zealous Charity

✦ **Does someone in the illuminative way practice the virtue of zeal for the spiritual life, social justice, or for doing God's will in all things?**

There seem to be two sides to the illuminative way, which is the experience of charity. One aspect is charity to our neighbor, and the other is the love of God. Zealous charity is manifest especially in concern for our neighbor. Those in the illuminative way will not count the cost of taking care of those in physical or spiritual need. They will attempt very difficult things, and surprisingly, they will usually succeed. The Catholic Church is filled with works of charity begun in extraordinary ways by extraordinary people. One need only consider the apostolic zeal of John Paul II, the incredible dedication of the two Capuchin friars, Padre Pio and Father Solanus Casey, and Mother Teresa's unwavering concern for others. This is zeal for the salvation for souls and the alleviation of human suffering. Interestingly enough, all four of these people spent their lives surrounded by surging crowds of people who endlessly intruded on their prayer and privacy, but they never seemed to lose the sense of God's presence. This shows great progress in the spiritual life. All four were probably in the unitive way toward the end of their lives, and yet they never withdrew from the care of souls. The same may be observed in the past among many saints of zealous charity: Vincent de Paul, Louise de Marillac, Don Bosco, and Mother Cabrini. The zeal of the Jesuit missionaries, like Edmund Campion and Isaac Jogues, demonstrates fidelity in the loving care of the faith of others despite the endurance of great deprivations.

✦ **Is the zeal we experience at the time of conversion a foretaste of the zeal we experience in the illuminative way? How do the two experiences differ? Is one more egotistical in nature?**

It may be said that one of the ways we can describe the spiritual life is to pass beyond ourselves. Early on, the dramatic phase "dying to self" may be used. That does not seem to make much sense, however, with those who are far advanced, because the self seems pretty much to have disappeared. What takes place is a growing experience of *agape*, or selfless love, which is seen in so many aspects of our Savior's life. For example, Our Lord speaks of His own selfless love and calls His followers to do the same in John 15:12–17. This passage should be the subject of frequent and careful meditation. Our Lord speaks of His own *kenosis*, or emptying of Himself. Before that, He spoke of the grain of wheat that falls to the ground and dies before it brings forth fruit. Those in the illuminative way are aware of a gradual relinquishing of self in many ways. This may involve a relinquishment not only of things that are morally wrong or even morally imperfect but also of the clinging to self. We have to give up not only bad things but also good things in the spiritual life. Confusion about this often troubles people who have made some progress. They are prepared to give up what is bad but not easily to give up what is good.

✦ **Do the light and joy experienced at the beginning of the illu-minative way refer to a new insight into the world and to a new purpose to all that exists?**

The illuminative way takes its name from the fact that it can be compared to an experience of light. Saint Augustine says, "You shone out and burned brightly and chased away my blindness." References to light are very common in writings about this stage of the spiritual journey. Enlightenment could refer to new insights into the meaning of life and human relationships, but it may be best to describe it as a light that reveals everything in one's possible view. It is almost like a flash of lightning. Lightning that strikes in a dark forest will illumine every leaf and pine needle for a split second. We often say things like, "I see that in a new light." Obviously this experience will fill a person with joy. Many difficulties and frustrations of life will suddenly have real meaning in terms of faith and hope. Others observing the changes in the person will think that it is simply an act of goodwill or virtue. Actually it is not an action on the individual's part at all, except for the fact that there is personal cooperation. It is a grace from above. To see things in the light of God is a gift of God, not a human accomplishment. In the Psalms we read "In thy light do we see light" (Psalm 36:9).

Presence of God

✦ **When someone's focus is on the presence of God in the illu-minative way, does that mean that he or she is likely to have an abiding sense that God is present in all things?**

The second stage of the illuminative way marks a movement into the unqualified period of charity, or love of God. This brings with it an awareness of God's presence and a willingness to do all things for Him. Anyone living in that state twenty-four hours a day would probably be overwhelmed and find it difficult to cope with life's everyday situations. The patience and endurance of good souls in the purgative way are often tested by those in the illuminative way. For that reason people in the illuminative way and in the unitive way are often misunderstood and badly treated. I have seen this happen in the case of those who are presented for beatification. An abiding sense of God's presence in all things is an immense grace, which is given only gradually. It is also true that those in the illuminative way can receive and respond to such a grace only gradually. There is a certain false sense of God's grace, a kind of self-hypnosis, which is occasionally evident among pseudomystics. Some people, having done some reading about the spiritual life, decide to make a personal career of it. Although possibly sincere, they vastly overestimate their level of holiness and advancement. They can be seen often with a silly grin on their faces. My only advice to anyone encountering such a person is: "Flee." Do not encourage pseudomystics in any way.

✦ **Can spiritual growth be fostered by the "practice of the presence of God," to use a term popularized by Brother Lawrence of the Resurrection?**

Brother Lawrence, a seventeenth-century Carmelite, was one of the first Catholic lay brothers to leave behind spiritual writings. They were for the most part letters he had written and interviews conducted by an informed priest. Millions of people have found these texts edifying and helpful from a humble soul who lived very much in God's presence. Whether we can teach ourselves his method is an interesting question. With the grace of the illuminative way we may find it easier to do this and in a more continuous way. We can certainly try to attend to God's presence in our lives. Beyond that, I think that in the case of Brother Lawrence we are dealing with an unusual grace of contemplation and an awareness of God's presence on a very high level. Such things are not learned through self-teaching. We grow in the spiritual life, make the sacrifices, meet the demands placed in our path. If such gifts as being powerfully aware of God's presence are given, we should accept them with the greatest humility and acknowledge that we did not cause the experience. In her years of spiritual darkness Blessed Teresa of Calcutta experienced God's presence as a thirst. She tried to teach the spirituality of thirst to others, especially the Missionaries of Charity. It is clearly not everyone's experience.

In my old age I have particular appreciation for Brother Lawrence's advice written to an elderly woman: "Let us live and die with God."

VI.

THE UNITIVE WAY

Unitive			
Dark Night of the Senses	Simple Union with God	Second Dark Night of the Soul	Transforming Union with God
	Gifts of Holy Spirit/ Beginning of Contemplation		Contemplation/ Simplicity of Prayer

✦ **What is the unitive way? Is it made up of stages?**

The unitive way, which is made up of various phases, is the highest level a human being can attain in this world. It does seem that the upper end of this stage is wide-open to infinity, so that we can never say that someone has achieved full union with God in this life, but there are very high states of this union.

It is not particularly helpful in a book like this to spend much time on the unitive way. If there are some people reading this book who are actually in the unitive way, they should close it immediately and start praying for the rest of us.

There is first of all the simple unitive way, in which the person lives with a powerful sense of being in God's presence and is filled with charity, zeal, and forgiveness of neighbor. An ease in forgiving is one of the by-products of the illuminative way.

Charity, zeal, and ease at prayer come to flower in the simple unitive way. Life is apparently very beautiful and filled with a sense of God's presence. We get some sense of the unitive way from some of the poetry of Saint Thérèse of Lisieux.

There is also what is called the transforming unitive way, in which the person moves into the highest regions of contemplation and self-giving. We can learn about these only by reading from the lives of people in that way, but they are often reticent to speak of it or let others know what profound favors they are receiving. If someone wishes to read about this, I would suggest the writings of Saints Teresa of Avila and John of the Cross, specifically his *Living Flame of Love*. This may, however, leave the reader completely confused and without an understanding of what the saint is talking about. If you feel that way, congratulations. You are not involved in self-deception. But it can be helpful to take a glance at the experiences of those who have reached the top of Mount Everest, even if you are still in the foothills. If we could actually listen to the prayer of those in the unitive way, we would probably be bored to death. It is nothing spectacular. God is not spectacular. God creates the heavens and the earth in silence. Looking up at the starry sky, we see a world of complete silence because there is no one present to hear the collision of the galaxies or the sound of the comets. Noise, chatter, even the wise writings of human beings fall to silence, as Saint Augustine tells us in his marvelous description of a contemplative moment with his mother at a window in Ostia. This is not meant to imply that they were already in the unitive way, but they seem to have had an intense contemplative experience for just a moment.

> If to any man the tumult of the flesh grew silent, silent the images of earth and sea and air: and if the heavens grew silent, and the very soul grew silent to herself and by not thinking of self mounted beyond self: if all dreams and imagined visions grew silent, and every

tongue and every sign and whatsoever is transient — for indeed if any man could hear them, he should hear them saying with one voice: We did not make ourselves, but He made us who abides forever: but if, having uttered this and so set us to listening to Him who made them, they all grew silent, and in their silence He alone spoke to us, not by them but by Himself: so that we should hear His word, not by any tongue of flesh nor the voice of an angel nor the sound of thunder nor in the darkness of a parable, but that we should hear Himself whom in all these things we love, should hear Himself and not them: just as we two had but now reached forth and in a flash of the mind attained to touch the eternal Wisdom which abides over all: and if this could continue, and all other visions so different be quite taken away, and this one should so ravish and absorb and wrap the beholder in inward joys that his life should eternally be such as that one moment of understanding for which we had been sighing — would not this be: "Enter Thou into the joy of Thy Lord?" But when shall it be? Shall it be when "we shall all rise again" and "shall not all be changed"?[20]

✦ Can someone who has reached the unitive way regress and lose spiritual ground?

Since our human free will is always operative, I suppose it is possible, although I do not know of any examples of that happening. It seems, moreover, that such a thing would be a complete catastrophe and probably precipitate despair or even the person's death. How could anyone live after having lost this high and beautiful place and return to the banality of worldliness at the bottom. Yet, there are people who have written rather eloquently about the spiritual life and then have become its enemy. A modern example is Bertrand Russell, who wrote a book called

Mysticism and Logic. He wrote about the spiritual life as someone who seemed to have understood, at least in its beginning stages. However, he became a strident atheist, openly espousing the persecution of religion. His case is rather frightening.

✦ What is the dark night of the soul?

We all experience darkness at times on the spiritual journey. It may come from external catastrophe, sorrows, the death of family members or friends, failure, sickness, or accidents. Paradoxically, these periods of darkness are meant to teach us to trust God. They may be prolonged, as in the case of those who endured occupation under the Nazis or Soviets. Darkness may also be completely personal and go unrecognized by others. Mother Teresa apparently lived in great spiritual darkness for thirty-five years. No one knew about it except her spiritual directors. Toward the end of the spiritual life, particularly during the passage from the illuminative to the unitive way, there seems to be an absolute stripping away by darkness. This happens with those who have given up everything to follow their awareness of God's presence. Suddenly God seems to disappear, and their love and zeal for God are tested. Darkness moves them from the enjoyment of God's presence to a point of selfless love, or *agape.* They remain faithful and true and complain to no one, or to a very limited number of spiritually informed people in order to get some support.

We all experience darkness on our way. Descriptions of the dark night by Saint John of the Cross make clear that like divine illumination, they are not just the ordinary experience of someone struggling on the spiritual journey.

✦ When someone has reached the unitive way, has he truly died to self and is he living for God alone?

It is difficult for someone who has not experienced the unitive way to speculate about it. My observation of those I believed with good evidence to be in the unitive way is that they had little or no self left. It was difficult to hurt or praise them, extol or argue with them, because they simply offered no resistance. Without some familiarity with a person in this stage of the spiritual life, it is almost impossible to conceive what it is like. It is something like working with a shadow. On the other hand, if they are asked to do something contrary to their conscience or their spiritual perceptions, they will not move. However, they are not aggressive or defensive in their refusal to move. There is always the evidence of a profound inner silence.

✦ **When we speak of dying to self, do we mean a complete loss of every last molecule of existence?**

It may be interesting to look at examples of people who in the midst of great suffering and even frightful circumstances did completely surrender to God. First, there is the death of Saint Joan of Arc, a young girl whose mystical visions changed the course of world history and ended the longest war in history. She followed what she believed to be a summons from God with simplicity and purity of heart. Winston Churchill, prime minister of the country she defeated, called her the purest figure in European history for a thousand years. Joan believed she was going to be released and not given up to the flames. She told that to a friendly inquisitor the day before. She said her voices told her not to be afraid of her martyrdom and that she would have a great victory. When the inquisitor asked her what the martyrdom meant, she said it referred to what she had suffered at their hands up to then. In fact, it was only as the flames rose around her that she realized she was not being delivered. She died very devoutly, repeating from the depth of her being the holy name of Jesus and indicating a complete surrender.

There is a similarity with the death of Saint Thérèse of Lisieux, who had written so beautifully of eternal life and then sank into great darkness and doubts against faith and hope. In the last moments of life she appears to have completely surrendered everything to God. It was the Sisters' impression that while still physically alive, she was passing into the eternal divine presence. These two examples may give us something to think about when we discuss the death to self. It does not happen suddenly and never completely, perhaps until the very end of life.

◆ **Do we have any modern examples of people who have arrived at this exalted level in the spiritual life?**

An example of someone closer to our time is Mother Teresa of Calcutta. I had the privilege of knowing her for thirty-two years. There was always a somberness about her that puzzled me. She had a sense of humor and was realistic, but she could also be very somber. Only after her death were her letters to her spiritual directors released. They revealed that she had lived in profound spiritual darkness, a burning thirst for God's presence, which she never doubted. Her motto was Christ's own words, "I thirst."

I had the opportunity of offering Mass for Mother Teresa on the day before she returned to India, six weeks before her death. She was a transformed person. I have used the word "bubbly" to describe her on that occasion. As we were leaving, I mentioned to my confrere Father Andrew that she was obviously going through the doors of death while she was still alive. It seemed to me that after thirty years of darkness she was then entering the divine light. I don't think it was completely accidental that I observed Mother Teresa at that time, because I was able to give this testimony during the process for her beatification.

Part Three

HELP FOR THE JOURNEY

VII.

SACRAMENTS, SACRIFICE, AND THE CHURCH

✦ **Is the celebration of the Holy Eucharist and reception of the sacrament of essential importance in our spiritual journey?**

For Catholics and Orthodox Christians, the Eucharist, the holy sacrifice that is liturgically celebrated every day — popularly known as the Mass by Catholics — is both an integral part and the center of the spiritual life. Other Christian communities, although they define the eucharistic celebration differently, do observe a communion of bread and wine, which they see, at least symbolically, as the presence of Christ among them.

For Catholics, Orthodox Christians, and some Anglicans and Lutherans, however, the Eucharist must have a focus that is not there for evangelical or other Christians because of a matter of belief. We must not see the Eucharist simply as a religious service. All world religions have public services of prayer to God and encouragement to their people, which are celebrated daily, or at least weekly. This is not what the Eucharist is.

In the succeeding paragraphs I will refer to the celebration and reception of the Eucharist either as the Mass or the liturgy. Liturgy comes from an ancient Greek word (*leitourgia*, meaning public service), and it is exclusively used in the Eastern churches, whereas Mass or liturgy is used in the West.

✦ **Doesn't the Mass, or liturgy, constitute simply public prayer to God?**

No. Liturgy is the re-presentation of the sacrifice of Christ and the sacrificial gift of Himself to the Father; by that gift of self He lovingly gives Himself to us and draws us into the divine life. Pope Benedict XVI has emphasized the ancient understanding of the liturgy revived by the Benedictine monks of Solesmes and Maria Laach in the nineteenth and early twentieth centuries. He has expressed the hope that this liturgical piety will reverse a confusing situation and introduce a profound understanding of the Eucharist. I highly recommend to any sacramental Christian the study of the Holy Father's exhortation *Sacramentum Caritatis* (Sacrament of Charity).[21]

The Pope points out that Christ is giving Himself as the Lamb of sacrifice at the ritual meal of the Jewish religion, which celebrated the liberation of the people from slavery.

> The remembrance of their ancient liberation thus expanded to the invocation and expectation of a yet more profound, radical, universal and definitive salvation. This is the context in which Jesus introduces the newness of His gift.... In instituting the sacrament of the Eucharist, Jesus anticipates and makes present the sacrifice of the Cross and the victory of the resurrection. At the same time, He reveals that He Himself is the *true* sacrificial lamb, destined in the Father's plan from the foundation of the world, as we read in the First Letter of Peter (see 1:18–20). By placing His gift in this context, Jesus shows the salvific meaning of His death and resurrection, a mystery which renews history and the whole cosmos. The institution of the Eucharist demonstrates how Jesus' death, for all its violence and absurdity,

became in Him a supreme act of love and mankind's definitive deliverance from evil.[22]

Saint Peter's words are so important that it would be well to memorize them:

> You know that you were ransomed from the futile ways inherited from your fathers, not with perishable things such as silver or gold, but with the precious blood of Christ, like that of a lamb without blemish or spot. He was destined before the foundation of the world but was made manifest at the end of the times for your sake (1 Peter 1:18–20).

✦ What does this theology tell us about the nature of the Church?

It tells us that the Church is something absolutely new, that it does not have a parallel in human history, any more than the Eucharistic sacrifice has a parallel. There are figures of the Church beforehand, like Israel, and figures of the Mass, like the sacrifice of the paschal lamb and the Passover meal of the Jews. Now, however, we have a reality which we are commanded by Christ to keep in remembrance of Him (see Luke 22:19). The Pope says:

> In these words the Lord expresses, as it were, his expectation that the Church, born of his sacrifice, will receive this gift, developing under the guidance of the Holy Spirit the liturgical form of the sacrament. The remembrance of his perfect gift consists not in the mere repetition of the Last Supper, but in the Eucharist itself, that is, in the radical newness of Christian worship. . . . "The Eucharist draws us into Jesus' act of self-oblation. More than just statically receiving the incarnate *Logos*, we

enter into the very dynamic of his self-giving." Jesus "draws us into himself."[23]

✦ Doesn't it seem that Pope Benedict gives a new interpretation to the meaning of the Mass?

The Holy Father gives the classic understanding of the Mass from the Church Fathers outlined very well in the opening paragraphs of *Sacramentum Caritatis*. The eucharistic Christian must meditate a good deal on the meaning of the liturgy and how the Church in its holiness and its everlasting significance as the Body of Christ is born of the suffering of Jesus in His "hour."

✦ Once we have grasped in some way the meaning of the Eucharist and the meaning of the Church born of the Eucharist, how is that to affect us in our spiritual life?

Devout and prayerful participation in the liturgy, especially on a daily basis, is extremely helpful. Most Catholics attempting to lead a devout life will almost instinctively include participation at daily Mass in their schedule. Pope Benedict teaches that this must be done with awe and reverence. (I began to attend daily Mass when I was fourteen years old.)

✦ How does Pope Benedict's understanding fit in with some of the popular explanations and attitudes about the liturgy current in recent decades?

Indeed, it is possible to hear an explanation of the Eucharist in church which does not come from the Church's traditional teaching and is quite garbled.

Some of our readers may be in circumstances in which it will be necessary to take up independent study and stand on their own. Unfortunately, education in Catholic universities and seminaries in recent decades became seriously diluted by rationalism and worldliness. Although during the same period many people expressed a desire for, and interest in, prayer of many different kinds — including such things as meditation groups and centering prayer — there was a neglect of the liturgy, caused by defective theological teachings, especially about the Eucharist. Believers must, therefore, work on their own in ways we have indicated so far, particularly through reading and, if possible, through study in authentic Catholic programs or with devout groups like the Oratory of Divine Love.[24]

✦ What is the central focus of liturgical piety?

Ultimately, it is the love of Christ expressed in the Eucharist at the Last Supper and then lived out in its fullness at Calvary and in His Resurrection. We can never come to the end of our meditations about, nor exhaust the depths of the mystery of Christ's love manifested in His suffering, death, and Resurrection. The *sacramentum caritatis* means attempting to live the Christian spiritual life we have been given by the gift of integral faith. Catholics or Orthodox Christians who do not make the Eucharist the center of their lives become, in effect, devout Evangelical Protestants, burdened, moreover, with what must seem like the trappings of clericalism. This is because people fail to distinguish between the externals of the Christian faith and their inner meaning. Anyone who reads the documents of the early Church Fathers, which form a continuous thread of teaching from the Gospel and Saint Paul's doctrine of the Eucharist, will realize that liturgy and the Eucharist are the heart of historically authentic Christian life. This does not detract from the sincerity of Evangelical Christians, but it does point out a regrettable absence in their lives. It is my impression that if Evangelical Christians had some understanding and valid contact with the Eucharist as the sacrament of charity, they would be the first to embrace it enthusiastically. In fact, I think that if Jewish people were able to appreciate the life of

Christ as presented in the Gospels and other New Testament writings, they would embrace the Eucharist, as Saint Teresa Benedicta of the Cross (Edith Stein) did in her own life.

✦ **Is it necessary to make a distinction in mind and practice between the liturgy and the center of the liturgy, which is the Eucharist?**

It may be helpful to do this. The liturgical forms that surround the mystery of Eucharist are developments of the Church. In fact, there are many accepted and valid liturgies in the Catholic Church. They range from the Roman rite, which most people identify as the single Catholic worship, to the Eastern rites and the very ancient rites, like the Ethiopian Coptic rite and the Syro-Malabar rite of India.

The liturgy, therefore, varies considerably in the external form of celebration. At its heart, however, is the obvious giving of oneself to Christ and, through Christ, to the Father, in union with His holy sacrifice of charity. He comes to us in the Mass and draws us to the Father with Him.

✦ **We must admit that we need to study the liturgy and live it more profoundly. However, what do we do if the liturgy is poorly celebrated?**

Pope Benedict has rightly said that Christians should always pray with reverence and awe. They should also pray with sufficient theological understanding that suits their own level of education and comprehension. We have already discussed how the *Catechism of the Catholic Church* may help them. Profound meditation on the meaning of the liturgy, using perhaps *Sacramentum Caritatis* or Pope John Paul II's encyclical *Ecclesia de Eucharistia*, is highly recommended. It is important to make a mental distinction between the liturgical ceremonies that traditionally and appropriately surround the mystery of the Eucharist and the mystery itself. It is so important to recall that even the celebrant's attitudes do not affect its validity and significance. It can be said that the Eucharist is the hands of the risen and infinite Christ reaching through time and space to bring to us again His sacrifice of love, by which He gained our salvation and opened for us the way to eternal life. This was Christ's way of giving ultimate glory to His Father, a glory that He had with the Father before the world began (see John 17:5; see also the entire Last Supper discourse in John 13–17).[25]

VIII.

SPIRITUAL DIRECTION

Perhaps the most challenging thought that follows upon a person's first religious conversion is the notion of seeking spiritual direction. The term itself is a bit off-putting. We will examine a few aspects of this part of the spiritual journey.

✦ **What does the term spiritual direction signify?**

Spiritual direction simply involves getting consistent and steady advice and teaching about the journey to God from the same informed person over a period of time. This definition is purposely general because there are many different ways and styles of spiritual direction.

✦ **Is it accurate to say that there seem to be few people around now who give spiritual direction?**

In the past, spiritual direction was seen almost exclusively as part of the clergy's role. It was considered one of the priest's pastoral responsibilities up until the time of the Council. This does not mean that other people, including religious sisters and brothers, did not give spiritual direction, particularly to members of their own communities. However, it was not called spiritual direction, because this was seen as being exclusively within the domain of clergy. In recent times large numbers of people — clergy, laity, and religious — have taken courses in how to give spiritual direction or at least as part of pastoral counseling. As a result of the impact of psychology and counseling on the Church in the early

1960s, spiritual direction began to look simply like pastoral counseling. In fact, the traditional roles almost reversed. Secular psychotherapists often took over the role of spiritual director, for which they had no training or competence at all. Spiritual direction as an art almost disappeared in the decade that followed. It has had something of a revival in recent years.

✦ What does it mean for someone to receive spiritual direction?

It means that someone experiencing the call of grace and trying to grow in the journey of the three ways seeks instruction and guidance, consciously or unconsciously, from someone else. Unfortunately, because of the shortage of clergy and the decline in the number of religious sisters and brothers, there is a dearth of spiritual directors at the present time. Providentially, a number of laypeople have taken on this role, but as with all things, they need to be well trained and instructed in what they are doing. Many readers of this book, in fact, may not know a single person whom they would identify as a spiritual director. If they approached their parish priest about receiving spiritual direction, he might be overwhelmed with work and unable to give the individual attention required.

✦ Given the shortage of priests and other qualified personnel, how is the average Catholic to receive spiritual direction?

One answer is to be found in appropriate religious, or spiritual, reading. The library of spiritual literature is vast, and some of it is effective in directing people in their spiritual journey. I intentionally set myself the goal many years ago to write books and give conferences that would give spiritual information and advice to others. In general, the books I have written are meant to be used for personal spiritual direction.

✦ How do we know if we can trust a particular spiritual director or spiritual writer to lead us in the proper direction?

This is an important issue. Church history reveals tragic examples of people who received erroneous spiritual direction and suffered considerably as a result. So great a person as Saint Teresa of Avila complains vigorously about the incompetence of some of the spiritual direction she received. Particularly dangerous at present are those interested in New Age spiritualities, or methods and insights that have not withstood the test of time. Some of those who would be most likely to present or advertise themselves as spiritual directors have caught on to a particular set of ideas or writings and are in fact promoters of a particular private revelation or insight or trendy technique. This is especially dangerous because people without adequate and broad training often do not know how to evaluate the accuracy and authenticity of a new set of ideas. It must be admitted in defense of ill-trained spiritual directors that the world of psychotherapy has had many examples of people who were trained in one technique and saw everything from that viewpoint. They did not, however, have the knowledge or inclination to examine it critically or to see other points of view. The same may also be said of certain forms of scholarship in Sacred Scripture that revealed a noticeable imbalance between contemporary theory and classical knowledge in the field. Pope Benedict XVI has pointed out this tendency in the preface to *Jesus of Nazareth*.

✦ What are some examples of the imbalance in psychotherapy and spiritual direction?

In the late 1950s and 1960s much attention was given to the psychological processes recommended by Carl Rogers and others who supported what was called client-directed therapy. No serious attempt was ever made to give firm intellectual foundations to this technique, although it appeared to work in many cases.

Because it was an easy technique to learn, many people, even those seeking training in spiritual direction, followed consciously and deliberately a nondirective model. Sometimes, as happened with a particular religious community in California, to whom Rogers and his associates gave a summer program, the results were nothing less than a disaster. When a new psychological method is used, it is important that the intellectual foundations and the verifiable insights of the method be carefully evaluated and understood. This is especially true when the technique is applied to spiritual direction.

Client-directed spiritual direction seems like a contradiction in terms, and often it was. Its first supposition, which is basically the heresy of Pelagius, was that the person holds within himself all the necessary ingredients of mental health and, in this case, of spiritual growth. There was an implicit denial of any need for the teachings of Scripture or the classic authors on the spiritual life and often a practical denial of any need for grace. Rogers himself seems to have been Pelagian, that is, someone who denies the effects of original sin. Consequently, if you followed the Rogerian model, you became the best edition of yourself, which was frequently a spiritual disaster and took a person far from the Gospel and the Church. Let it be said, however, that it was never the conscious intention of Rogerians to do this, even though the idea of conversion appears to have been almost completely missing from their approach.

Other models of therapy became incorporated into spiritual direction and were often new wine put into old wineskins (see Matthew 9:17). At the present time there is an emphasis on the need for virtue for psychological growth and mental health, which is certainly a move in the right direction. The proponents of this system, however, led by Professor Martin Seligman, have practically no experience of the spiritual life and a limited understanding of the scriptural teachings on virtue.[26] They have indeed opened a door, but an examination of their method, which is very welcome, shows that they themselves are honestly working to understand what virtue is and what its component character strengths are.

✦ Given all of the dangers, is it better not to get involved with spiritual direction?

No. That could be limiting the Providence of God. The best thing is to have a good spiritual director who is both trained and enlightened in the teaching of the Christian faith. If that cannot be done, there are some other possibilities.

✦ What are these possibilities?

As indicated already, one significant substitute for having a spiritual director is good solid spiritual reading. It should be expressly guided by the Scriptures and the Church's teaching and tradition and directed toward growing in the spiritual life. Another alternative is to seek out preachers and speakers who attempt to give group spiritual direction, and they are often very well received because people are so hungry for spiritual nourishment. Another substitute for a spiritual director is a spiritual friend or friends who are companions along the way.

✦ What do the terms "spiritual friend or companion" mean?

We all know people who share our spiritual interests and goals. They are sometimes gifted with much common sense and are reasonably well read in the spiritual life. It is a good idea occasionally to bounce ideas off another person. It has been recommended in recent decades to have an individual or group with whom to travel spiritually. This is part of many lay organizations, which have a particular spirituality. While there are too many to list here, they range from the Focolare movement to Opus Dei, and from Regnum Christi to the Oratory of Divine Love and Communion and Liberation (*Comunione e Liberazione*). Such movements provide spiritual direction for individuals and groups. Anyone belonging to a strongly motivated group should bear in mind that the primary group established by Jesus Christ is the Catholic Church. First and foremost one must be loyal to the Church. It goes without saying that whatever is done must be in keeping with the teaching of the Church and the Holy Father.

✦ What part does confession play in spiritual direction?

Given the shortage of priests, it is a good idea to have a regular confessor, that is, a priest to whom one habitually confesses. The penitent should not be defensive in confession, and a good confessor can come to grips with questions and problems more quickly than he can in a counseling situation. In the many years I have taught in seminaries I have tried to assist seminarians to realize what a marvelous work it is to hear confessions. For many, their only spiritual direction comes from the priest in confession. Non-Catholics who do not have any opportunity for the sacrament of reconciliation (confession) should realize that many of their clergy do something approximating the hearing of confessions. While not a sacramental encounter, it provides an opportunity for spiritual direction. I wish that such a confidential examination of one's conscience and sins would become more common in the devout Protestant world.

One of the tasks the spiritual director performs is to discover where someone is on the spiritual road. He also advises people when they are off the track, taking detours, and wasting much time and energy. The director can also effectively tell people that because of difficulties and dryness, they have fallen somewhat behind and that they should return with enthusiasm to their spiritual pursuits. A spiritual director can be a tremendous help to people in time of darkness, as can be seen in Mother Teresa's letters to her spiritual directors during her times of aridity and trial.

✦ **What can we do in the absence of any other source of spiritual direction except reading or televised sermons and teaching, such as we see on EWTN?**

First, give careful to attention to the selection of reading. Listen to teachers and preachers whose obvious goal is to help people spiritually — this is the goal of many programs currently on EWTN. The ultimate answer, however, is to rely humbly and patiently on the Holy Spirit. He is our ultimate spiritual director. If we trust Him and allow Him to lead us along the way, if we are not headstrong or determined to decide beforehand what His will is, He enters gently into our lives and guides us each day although we may hardly notice. Truly He is our spiritual director. This is Our Lord's meaning when He tells us: "[T]he Counselor, the Holy Spirit, whom the Father will send in my name, he will teach you all things, and bring to your remembrance all that I have said to you" (John 14:26).

IX.

SPIRITUAL READING

✦ **What is spiritual reading?**

It is not simply the reading of religious subjects, which might be done in weekly or monthly Catholic periodicals. Spiritual reading is a serious and purposeful meditative reading of texts on the spiritual life that cover a variety of areas of importance. Because of the immense body of literature on Christian and Catholic spiritual life, it is important to have some guides in this area. The following outline may be helpful in sorting out the precious but somewhat daunting collection of writings.

✦ **We have already spoken of Sacred Scripture. What about writings concerning the Scriptures?**

Theologians and scholars have been writing about the Scriptures since the Church's earliest days. We see their writings often in the Liturgy of the Hours and in other places. A number of Church Fathers wrote extensive commentaries especially on the Gospels and the Psalms. In modern times there have been writings on the Scriptures by scholars whose main focus seems to be on linguistics, that is, on the exact meaning of each word and the overall translation. They are concerned with how the original text was understood by the human author. This can be an extremely complex area of study and can leave the reader confused and stuck in the past.

Readers should certainly be informed on the meaning of Scripture through the use of a good commentary. As mentioned above, however, care must be taken to avoid those inclining to skepticism and rationalism.[27]

✦ What about reading theology?

Most theological books are not written for spiritual guidance, but rather are cast objectively in the framework of study. In recent years writings of Pope John Paul II and Pope Benedict XVI have departed from the model of cold theological study in their writings.

We have mentioned some of the theological writers of the first half of the twentieth century like Abbot Marmion and Msgr. Guardini, whose purpose was to inform those who were not trained theologians about the profound spiritual significance of Christian doctrine. Although the *Catechism of the Catholic Church* is written in a rather objective way, the authors obviously intended that it edify as well as educate the reader. The *Compendium* makes the *Catechism* a little easier to read.[28]

✦ Are there any books to instruct us how to make progress in the spiritual life?

Such books are generally referred to as spiritual reading and include many great classic works of the past. In any list the following must be included: the *Confessions* of Saint Augustine; *The Imitation of Christ*; *Introduction to the Devout Life*, of Saint Francis de Sales; the autobiographies of Saints Teresa of Avila and Thérèse of Lisieux.

In addition, there are a number of books written in the nineteenth and early twentieth centuries by those who were interested in giving spiritual direction: John Henry Newman (1801–1890); Father Frederick William Faber (1814–1863), of the London Oratory; Archbishop Alban Goodier, S.J., and others.[29]

By mid-twentieth century the books of Bishop Fulton Sheen were becoming popular, and since the Second World War tremendous interest in the spiritual life has been sparked by Thomas Merton. From his writings, particularly the *Seven-Storey Mountain*, as well as *Seeds of Contemplation*, came a whole literature of personal spirituality reflecting contemplation. A remarkable number of books were written in the last decades of the twentieth century — some of them good, many of them superficial — including those of Carlo Carretto; Raniero Cantalamessa, O.F.M. Cap.; Father George Maloney, S.J.; Henri Nouwen; and Father Adrian van Kaam and Susan Muto, whose works were more psychological but still had a strong spiritual component. Members of the charismatic renewal also did much spiritual writing, some of which was specific to their movement. Others moved into the mainstream of Catholic life, for instance, Ralph Martin's book *The Fulfillment of All Desire*. Although Scott Hahn's books tend to deal with apologetics, they also provide a great deal of thought about the spiritual life.

✦ **How does someone select books that are personally appropriate?**

First, several questions must be asked. What am I looking for? Do I want someone to tell me the steps of the spiritual life, as we have done in this book? Do I want insight and inspiration about the Christian mysteries and life? Do I want to read something that will give me a strong sense of purpose and direction in my responsibilities to my fellow human beings? Do I want something that will provide consolation and help in dark times? These and other questions can serve as a guide in the selection of books.

✦ **Is there a list of such appropriate books?**

Readers will find a brief bibliography at the end of this book indicating contemporary publishers whose works can be ordered online. It would be a good idea for those who have access to a good Catholic college or seminary library to wander through the sections on Christian teaching and the spiritual life. Books are often a matter of taste and inclination; those that appeal to some will not elicit much response in others. Many people have been introduced to several authors who might otherwise have remained obscure through Paulist Press's series, the Classics of Western Spirituality.

CONCLUSION

✦ **As we come to the end of our questions, can we make any general observations about the spiritual life, given the present situation in the Church and in our culture?**

This book is written in the firm hope that we have come to the end of what has been one of the great crises in Catholic history, certainly in the United States. Other Christian denominations have suffered somewhat from the fallout of this crisis, but they too are struggling with the impact of skeptical approaches to Sacred Scripture and the effects of the worldly and negative culture, or anticulture, that surrounds us. In a word, these are not easy times for spiritual people.

It should be recalled, however, that every circumstance in human life offers the believer the opportunity to grow and bring Christ's grace to life's challenges. As Saint Thérèse observed, echoing Saint Paul, "Everything is grace." This powerful part of Christianity begins with Christ's words: "If any man would come after me, let him deny himself and take up his cross and follow me" (Mark 8:34); and again, "Whoever does not bear his own cross and come after me, cannot be my disciple" (Luke 14:27). These words can be said in a somber, challenging way, but they can also be interpreted extremely positively. If we take up the cross and follow Christ, we will find blessings and opportunities to come closer to God in whatever happens. We see this in Christ's crucifixion and death. His horribly unjust ignominy resulted in the Resurrection and the salvation of the world. The same theme is repeated, much less dramatically, in the life of every disciple of Christ. Whatever is going on — blessings or difficult times —

gives us the opportunity to apply Christ's Gospel, to live according to it, and to bring light into the darkness.

Today's disciples of Christ, therefore, should not become discouraged. By God's Providence we have been chosen to live in these times and bring His grace to situations we live in and the people we meet. Waste no time on wishing to have lived in another age. Even though we may disapprove of much in our own day, we must love our times in the sense that we bring Christ's message in different ways to this time in history.

Saint Catherine of Siena is said to have had visions of hell and symbolic trips through the place of lost souls. At one point she saw a burning island crowded with people and asked her guide who they were. She was told that it was the place of those who did not love their own time.

She was a great reformer and critic of what went on in her day. She changed Church history in a seemingly impossible situation. She had tremendous faith and trust and especially a burning love for Jesus Christ and His Church.

Throughout history many great Christians lived in what must be called bad times. They brought the Gospel message to those times. If we live in bad times, each of us will do this differently. Some will do it quietly, others with much attention. Some will do it through works of compassion and charity, others by prayer. Disciples of Christ should do it by whatever means are available.

As I bring this guide to a conclusion, I make a fervent appeal that we not simply explore the spiritual life with all its ramifications and religious traditions. Most of all we are called to be disciples of Our Lord Jesus Christ, the carpenter of Nazareth, the preacher of the kingdom of God, the victim of the Cross, the victor of the Resurrection, the one who will come to judge the living and the dead. That final work of Christ is our goal, and the whole of what we do must be seen in the light of His coming again.

ACKNOWLEDGMENTS

As I completed this book, I was more aware than ever of the immense debt I owe to the spiritual writers of the Christian tradition and of other traditions where the spiritual life is seriously discussed and explored. I am particularly grateful to those who have contributed to the immense library of Catholic spiritual writing.

I want to thank my friend and associate Charles Pendergast for his invaluable help in preparing the manuscript and in assisting me amid a great number of other duties that claim my attention. I express my gratitude also to Michael Dubruiel, of Our Sunday Visitor, whose idea it was to do a book in this format and who provided many useful suggestions.

Let us pray for one another.

NOTES

---

[1] See Christopher Peterson and Martin Seligman, *Character Strengths and Virtues: A Handbook and Classification* (Oxford University Press, 2004).

[2] This question is dealt with at length in **VII. Sacraments, Sacrifice, and the Church** on pages 99-105.

[3] See *Story of a Soul*. Several translations are available, including the ICS edition, 1999.

[4] This question is dealt with at length in **VIII. Spiritual Direction** on pages 107-113.

[5] (Crossroad, 1982; reprinted 2000).

[6] See *Catherine of Genoa: Purgation and Purgatory, The Spiritual Dialogue*, trans. Serge Hughes. Introduction by Benedict J. Groeschel (New York: Paulist Press, 1979).

[7] See Mary C. Darrah, *Sister Ignatia: Angel of Alcoholics Anonymous* (2nd edition, Hazelden, 2001).

[8] I attempted to refound this series of prayer groups for laypeople in 2003 and bring back the opportunity for prayer and devout study among serious Christians.

[9] See Father Benedict J. Groeschel, C.F.R., *Praying with the Creed: Meditations from the Oratory* (OSV, 2007).

[10] The books of Scott Hahn would fit into the first category, while the *Confessions* of Saint Augustine and the works of Thomas Merton, particularly *The Seven-Storey Mountain*, would fall into the second. A bibliography of spiritual classics is given at the end of this book.

[11] Doubleday, 2007.

[12] See the 1982 Regnery edition with Introduction by Joseph Cardinal Ratzinger.

[13] *The Companion to the* Catechism of the Catholic Church (Ignatius Press, 1994) is a helpful volume to have at hand when studying the *Catechism*. Some commentaries on the *Catechism*, however, are, unfortunately, negative and confusing. Caution must be used in this area.

[14] Lincoln Barnett, *The Universe and Dr. Einstein*, with introduction by Albert Einstein (New York: William Morrow and Company, 1948), 105.

[15] OSV, 2005.

[16] "The Hind and the Panther," Part I.

[17] Fr. Louis Lallemant, S.J., *La Doctrine spirituelle*, chapter 6, cited in Rev. R. Garrigou-Lagrange, O.P., *The Three Ages of the Interior Life*, II, trans. Sr. M. Timothea Doyle, O.P. (Rockford, Ill.: Tan Books and Publishers, 1989), 23.

[18] *La Doctrine spirituelle*, chapter 2, in Ibid., 26.

[19] Ibid., 43ff. See also St. John of the Cross, *Dark Night of the Soul*, Book I, chapter 10.

[20] St. Augustine, *Confessions*, trans. Frank Sheed, Book Nine, x.

[21] See edition published by Pauline Books & Media, 2007. See also Vatican website (www.vatican.va).

[22] *Sacramentum Caritatis*, 10.

[23] Ibid., 11.

[24] For more information on the Oratory of Divine Love visit their website at: www.oratorydl.org

[25] There are many worthwhile books on the subject of liturgy. See, for example: Joseph Cardinal Ratzinger, *The Spirit of the Liturgy* (Ignatius Press, 2000); Pope Pius XII's encyclical *Mediator Dei*; Abbot Columba Marmion, *Christ in His Mysteries* (unfortunately out of print, but available in any good Catholic library); and Scott Hahn, *The Lamb's Supper* (Doubleday, 1999).

[26] See Paul C. Vitz, "Psychology in Recovery," *First Things* 151 (March 2005): 17–22.

[27] See Pope Benedict XVI, *Jesus of Nazareth*, which provides not only guidance in the reading of scripture scholars and commentators but also a rich and learned study of the life of Christ from a theological point of view.

[28] *Compendium of the Catechism of the Catholic Church* (USCCB, 2005).

[29] It may be argued that Newman's works — like his treatises on the Apostolic Fathers — fall into the category of objective theological study rather than of spiritual direction. However, his Sunday homilies (sermons) at St. Mary's, his grasp of Sacred Scripture, and his always sage advice on the pursuit of Christian perfection, make much of his *corpus* ready nourishment for the spiritual life. Moreover, he has so rapidly taken his place, like Augustine and Aquinas, as the greatest man of his age that no Catholic could consider himself well informed if he has not read at least some Newman.

A BIBLIOGRAPHY FOR BEGINNERS

BOOKS ON THE SPIRITUAL LIFE

Cantalamessa, O.F.M. Cap., Raniero. *Contemplating the Trinity.* Word Among Us Press, 2007.

_____. *The Holy Spirit in the Life of Jesus.* Liturgical Press, 1994.

_____. *Jesus Christ, the Holy One of God.* Liturgical Press, 1991.

_____. *Loving the Church.* Servant Publications, 2005.

Chautard, O.C.S.O., Jean-Baptiste. *The Soul of the Apostolate.* Tan Books and Publishers, 1977.

Dubay, S.M., Thomas. *Fire Within.* Ignatius Press, 1989.

_____. *Prayer Primer: Igniting a Fire Within.* Charis Books, 2002.

_____. *Seeking Spiritual Direction: How to Grow the Divine Life Within.* Servant Publications, 1994.

Garrigou-Lagrange, O.P., Reginald. *Christian Perfection and Contemplation.* Translated by Sister M. Timothea Doyle, O.P. Kessinger Publishing, 2007.

_____. *The Mother of the Savior and our Interior Life.* Tan Books and Publishers, 1994.

_____. *The Three Ages of the Interior Life.* Translated by Sister M. Timothea Doyle, O.P. Tan Books and Publishers, 1989.

Groeschel, Benedict. *Spiritual Passages: The Psychology of Spiritual Development.* Crossroad, 2000.

_____. *Listening at Prayer.* Paulist Press, 1984.

Hahn, Scott. *The Lamb's Supper: The Mass as Heaven on Earth.* Doubleday, 1999.

von Hildebrand, Dietrich. *Transformation in Christ*. Ignatius Press, 2001.

_____. *The Heart: An Analysis of Human and Divine Affectivity*. St. Augustine Press, 2007.

Marmion, Blessed Columba. *Union with God: Letters of Spiritual Direction by Blessed Columba Marmion*. Zaccheus Press, 2006.

Ratzinger, Joseph. *The Spirit of the Liturgy*. Translated by John Saward. Ignatius Press, 2000.

_____. *Called to Communion: Understanding the Church Today*. Translated by Adrian Walker. Ignatius Press, 1996.

Sheen, Fulton J. *The World's First Love*. Ignatius Press, 1996.

_____. *The Seven Capital Sins*. Alba House, 2000.

Underhill, Evelyn. *Mysticism*. Dover Publications, 2002.

BOOKS ON THE LIFE OF CHRIST AND SCRIPTURE

Boylan, O.C.R., Eugene. *This Tremendous Lover*. Christian Classics, 1987.

Goodier, S.J., Alban. *The Meaning of Life: The Catholic Answer*. Sophia Institute Press, 1992.

_____. *Spiritual Excellence: How to Make Progress in Prayer and Love*. Sophia Institute Press, 2002.

Guardini, Romano. *The Lord*. Translated by Elinor Castendyk Briefs. Gateway, 2001.

Hahn, Scott: *A Father Who Keeps His Promises: God's Covenant Love in Scripture*. Servant Publications, 1998.

Marmion, Blessed Columba. *Christ, the Life of the Soul*. Zaccheus Press, 2005.

Ratzinger, Joseph. Pope Benedict XVI. *Jesus of Nazareth*. Translated from the German by Adrian J. Walker. Doubleday, 2007.

_____. *Behold the Pierced One*. Ignatius Press, 1987.

_____. *The Apostles: the Origin of the Church and Their Co-Workers*. OSV, 2007.

Sheen, Fulton J. *Life of Christ* (reprint). Image Books, 1977.

_____. *The Seven Last Words.* Alba House, 1996.

BOOKS ON PERSONAL PRAYER
AND DEVOTION

Caussade, S.J., Père Jean-Pierre de. *Self-Abandonment to Divine Providence.* Translated by Algar Thorold. St. Benedict Press, 2006.

Groeschel, Benedict with Kevin Perrotta. *The Journey Toward God.* Servant Publications, 2000.

Julian of Norwich. *The Revelation of Divine Love.* Liguori Publications, 1994.

Kempis, Thomas à. *The Imitation of Christ.* Translated by Ronald Knox and Michael Oakley. Ignatius Press, 2005.

Br. Lawrence of the Resurrection. *The Practice of the Presence of God.* Translated by Salvatore Sciurba, O.C.D. ICS Publications, 1994.

Martin, Ralph. *The Fulfillment of All Desire.* Emmaus Road, 2006.

Merton, Thomas. *Contemplative Prayer.* Image, 1971.

CLASSICS OF THE SPIRITUAL LIFE

Augustine of Hippo. *Confessions.* Translated by Frank Sheed. 2nd revised ed. Hackett Publishing, 2007.

Cloud of Unknowing, The. ed. James Walsh, S.J. Paulist Press, 1981.

St. Francis de Sales. *Introduction to the Devout Life.* St. Benedict Press, 2006.

_____. *Treatise on the Love of God.* Tan Books and Publishers, 1997.

St. John of the Cross. *The Collected Works of St. John of the Cross.* Translated by Kieran Kavanaugh, O.C.D. and Otilio Rodriguez, O.C.D. ICS Publications, 2001.

Newman, John Henry. *Apologia pro Vita Sua.* Kessinger Publishing, 2004.

_____. *Selected Sermons*. Paulist Press, 1994.

Przywara, Erich, S.J. *The Heart of Newman*. Ignatius Press, 1997.

St. Teresa of Avila. *Book of Her Life*, in *The Collected Works of St. Teresa of Avila*, vol. 1. Translated by Kieran Kavanaugh, O.C.D. and Otilio Rodriguez, O.C.D. ICS Publications, 1976.

_____. *Way of Perfection*, in *The Collected Works of St. Teresa of Avila*, vol. 2. Translated by Kieran Kavanaugh, O.C.D. and Otilio Rodriguez, O.C.D. ICS Publications, 1976.

St. Thérèse of Lisieux. *Story of a Soul*. Translated by John Clarke. ICS Publications, 1996.

BIOGRAPHY

There are innumerable biographies and studies of great people of the interior life. We list only a few here, but readers are encouraged to seek out others.

Görres, Ida Friederike. *The Hidden Face*. Ignatius Press, 2003.

Honoré, Jean. *The Spiritual Journey of Newman*. Alba House, 1992.

Ker, Ian. *John Henry Newman: A Biography*. Oxford University Press, 1990.

Merton, Thomas. *The Seven-Storey Mountain*. Harcourt, 1998.

NON-CATHOLIC

There are also many fine books on the spiritual life by Protestant and Orthodox authors. I do not feel competent to make a selection. Protestant spiritual writers range over the centuries from John Bunyan's *The Pilgrim's Progress* to contemporary writers like Billy Graham, Chuck Colson, and Elisabeth Elliot.

An excellent selection of Orthodox writers ancient and modern can be found in the bibliography given in *The Orthodox Way*, by Bishop Kallistos Ware (St. Vladimir's Seminary Press, 1999).